TRUE CRIME
Diary

TRUE CRIME
Diary

180 True Crime Stories

James Bland

WARNER BOOKS

A *Warner* Book

Copyright © James Bland 1986

The right of James Bland to be identified as author of
this work has been asserted by him in accordance with the
Copyright, Designs and Patents Act 1988.

First published in Great Britain in 1987
by Futura Publications
Reprinted 1987 (twice), 1988, 1989, 1990 (twice), 1992
This edition published by Warner Books in 1992
Reprinted 1992, 1993, 1994, 1996, 1998, 1999

A CIP catalogue record for this book
is available from the British Library.

ISBN 0 7515 9338 X

Printed in England by Clays Ltd, St Ives plc

Acknowledgements
Almost all the stories in this book were
originally published in the magazines *True Crime Monthly*,
True Detective and *Master Detective*

UK companies, institutions and other organisations wishing
to make bulk purchases of this or any other books
published by Little, Brown should contact their local
bookshop or the special sales department at the address below.
Tel 0171 911 8000. Fax 0171 911 8100.

Warner Books
A Division of
Little, Brown and Company (UK)
Brettenham House
Lancaster Place
London WC2E 7EN

CONTENTS

PREFACE

True Crime Diary recounts a large number of modern murder stories, many of them already famous. The subjects have been chosen according to my own preferences, with due regard for variety, oddities of character and quirks of fate. It is, as far as I know, the first time that such a collection has been arranged as a book of anniversaries, though about a third of the contents were originally published as a series with the same title in *True Crime Monthly*.

I have no doubt that some readers will notice discrepancies between my own accounts of certain cases and those currently available by other authors. This is always irritating to anyone with a keen interest in the subject, and it must be admitted that some authors in this field are not above presenting fiction as fact. As I do not wish to be regarded as one of them, I feel obliged to say that I have confined myself to using information which I believe to be accurate and that if I have erred at all, I have done so in good faith.

I make no apology for the fact that some of the stories are shocking, for nobody acquainted with the subject would expect otherwise. It is not only the cases of mass murder to which I am referring; many others, such as those of the Papin Sisters or Dr Geza de Kaplany, were so horrifying as to be incomprehensible to any normal person. I have no fresh insights or theories to offer in respect of such crimes; as with all the other cases, I have been content to describe them in a concise and, I hope, interesting manner. If the reader finds them absorbing, then the book is as I intended it to be.

Inquest on Margaret Lofty, 1915

On 1 January 1915, a man calling himself John Lloyd and claiming to be an estate agent told a London coroner's court of the tragic death of his wife, Margaret Elizabeth Lloyd, formerly Lofty, in a house in Highgate fourteen days earlier.

Weeping copiously, he said that on the day before her death he and his wife had moved into rooms at 14, Bismarck Road after travelling from Bath, where they had just been married. He had found her lying dead in the bathroom when he returned to the house after going out to buy some tomatoes.

A local doctor, who had been called to the house, told the court that Mrs Lloyd's death had been caused by drowning, and suggested that she had fainted as a result of getting into a hot bath while she was suffering from influenza.

The coroner's jury, having no reason to suspect foul play, accepted this explanation and brought in a verdict of death by misadventure. But that was not the end of the matter.

A report of the inquest, published in the *News of the World*, was read by a Buckinghamshire fruit-grower, Charles Burnham, whose daughter Alice had died in similar circumstances in Blackpool a year earlier, after marrying a man named George Smith. This George Smith, who claimed to be a bachelor of independent means, had insured Alice Burnham's life for £500 on the day before the marriage. Burnham informed the police that he suspected that George Smith and John Lloyd were the same person. As a result, an extensive investigation was started, and Charles Burnham's suspicions soon proved to be justified.

Moreover, a third case came to light — that of Beatrice

9

Williams, formerly Mundy, who had died in almost identical circumstances in Herne Bay in July 1912. Her husband, who called himself Henry Williams and claimed to be a picture-restorer, had gained £2500 by her death. Henry Williams was now also found to have been George Smith.

Margaret Lloyd's life had been insured for £700, and she had made a will in her husband's favour just a few hours before her death

On 23 March 1915, following police inquiries in many towns, George Joseph Smith, aged forty-three, was charged with three murders. At his trial on one of those charges, which began at the Old Bailey on 22 June, 112 witnesses and 264 exhibits were produced. Smith was shown to be a callous, predatory individual, who had committed bigamy several times in order to deprive lonely or unhappy women of their savings, and no one was left in any doubt that he was also a murderer.

In a demonstration of how he could have drowned his victims without leaving any signs of a struggle, a nurse was placed in a bath and pulled under the water by her feet. The rushing of water into her nasal passages produced immediate unconsciousness, and she had to be revived by artificial respiration.

Despite frequent outbursts, Smith was convicted and sentenced to death. He was hanged at Maidstone Prison on 13 August 1915.

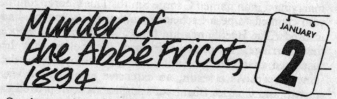

Murder of the Abbé Fricot, 1894

JANUARY 2

On the evening of 2 January 1894, the Abbé Fricot, rector of the parish of Entrammes, near Laval, sat down to make up his accounts in the company of his curate, the Abbé Albert Bruneau. What passed between the two priests is not known for certain, but it was clearly of some importance. At half past six a choir practice was cancelled without notice, the choir having already turned up at the rectory. Half an hour later, on being told that supper was ready, Bruneau said that Fricot had gone out. He then began playing the organ before going to have supper on his own. Though he appeared shaken at this point, it was also noticed that he had a good appetite. Later, when Fricot had still not appeared, a search of the premises was started, with neighbours being called in to help.

The search went on all night to no avail. In the morning Bruneau suggested that Fricot might have committed suicide and led his neighbour, a man named Chelle, to a well in the garden. There, under thirty feet of water, and concealed by logs, lay the body of the missing rector; his head had been battered with a heavy instrument. There were bloodstains on the edge of the well.

Bruneau was immediately suspected of the murder. His hand had been cut, but he claimed this had happened as he looked into the well at three o'clock in the morning, before leading Chelle to it. But there were also bloodstains on the keys of the organ, which Bruneau had played the previous evening. In his desk were found 1300 francs, which he appeared to have stolen from the rector's strong-box. A nun who visited the rectory had been told by Bruneau that Fricot had committed suicide — a mortal sin — and that his death had been made to look like murder in order to avoid a scandal.

Bruneau's character could hardly have helped to allay suspicion. A man of peasant origin, he was found to be a liar, a thief and a frequenter of brothels — at one of which he had contracted gonorrhoea. He had been a curate in Astillé, in the same province, for some years and during that time had used a bequest of 16,000 francs, intended for charity, for his own purposes. It was also while he was there that the rectory was burgled four times. He had

11

taken up his post in Entrammes at the age of thirty-one in November 1892, his arrival being quickly followed by the theft of 500 francs from a strong-box. It is likely that Fricot knew Bruneau to be the thief.

Neighbours claimed that on the night of the rector's death they heard groans coming from the rectory garden. It was supposed that Fricot, in making up his accounts, had decided that something had to be done about his curate's criminal activities, and that Bruneau had killed him after hearing what Fricot had to say on the matter.

Bruneau was brought to trial on 9 July. His sordid past was exposed, with prostitutes telling the court that he was a regular customer, and a brothel-keeper stating that he was not the only priest to turn up at her premises wearing his cassock. He was found guilty and sentenced to death, his execution on 29 August 1894, being attended by 16000 people. He died with dignity, declaring his innocence to the last.

Last murder by the Boston strangler, 1964

JANUARY
4

On 4 January 1964, the man known as the Boston Strangler committed his last murder. The body of the victim, Mary Sullivan, aged nineteen, was found in a Boston apartment. She had been stripped naked, tied up, raped and strangled; finally, a broom handle had been thrust into her body and, as a cruel act of mockery, a New Year greetings card placed against her right foot. Albert DeSalvo, a non-drinking, non-smoking schizophrenic with uncontrollable sexual urges, later confessed to being the Strangler. He was to remember that as Mary Sullivan lay dead 'she was looking like she was surprised and even disappointed with the way I had treated her'.

It was his thirteenth murder in just over eighteen months, though at the time it was believed to be only his eleventh, the other two not having been attributed to him. His victims had all been women and, though several were either elderly or middle-aged, all had been raped or sexually abused. He gained admission to their homes by posing as a workman, and invariably managed to avoid leaving fingerprints. Generally, the weapon he used was a ligature made from stockings, its ends being left in a bow under the victim's chin. Some of the victims were also found to have been beaten over the head, stabbed or bitten.

As the pattern became familiar, public tension mounted. The police searched their records for known sexual deviants and questioned many suspects, but they received only false confessions. One woman, in February 1963, had successfully fought off the Strangler, but was suffering from a partial loss of memory as a result of her ordeal. After the death of Mary Sullivan, when the murders suddenly stopped, it was feared that the culprit would never be caught.

Then, on 27 October the same year, a young married woman in Cambridge, Massachusetts, was tied up and sexually assaulted by an intruder. The description she gave of him led police to DeSalvo, who had a record for break-ing and entering. This, in turn, led to his photograph being circulated to neighbouring states, with the result that scores of women, all victims of sex attacks, identified him as their assailant. But DeSalvo, even then, was not suspected of being the Strangler. Held on rape charges, he was sent to the Boston State Hospital at Bridgewater for observation. On 4 February 1965, after confessing to a great many crimes, he was judged to be not competent to stand trial and committed to the hospital by court order. It was only then that he confessed to being the Strangler.

He gave details of the murders, in some cases making a sketch of the victim's home. He demonstrated the knot he

13

had used when strangling his victims. But the police, while convinced that he was telling them the truth, could not find any evidence to support his confessions. The state therefore reached an agreement with DeSalvo's attorney that no charges would be brought in connection with the murders, but that DeSalvo would be brought to trial for some of his other crimes instead.

The hearing began on 30 June 1966, with reporters and other observers from all over the world present. At the end of it DeSalvo, pleading for medical treatment, was sent to prison for life. In 1973, at the age of forty-two, he was stabbed to death by a fellow prisoner in Walpole State Prison.

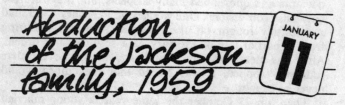

Abduction of the Jackson family, 1959

JANUARY 11

On 11 January 1959, Carrol Jackson, driving along a road near Apple Grove, Eastern Virginia, with his wife and two little daughters — one aged five, the other eighteen months — was forced to a halt by the driver of an old blue Chevrolet who had pulled over in front of them and stopped suddenly. Before Jackson could reverse and drive away, the other driver jumped out into the road and, threatening them with a gun, made the whole family get into the trunk of his own car. Later, when Jackson's car was found abandoned, a police search started, but no member of the missing family was to be seen alive again.

The bodies of Jackson and the younger girl were found in a ditch near Fredericksburg seven weeks later; Jackson had been shot in the head, the child had died of suffocation lying underneath him. Seventeen days after that the other two members of the family were found in a shallow grave near Annapolis, Maryland; the mother had been raped and murdered, the child beaten to death with a blunt instrument. The grave was not far from the place where another woman had been shot dead and then sexually assaulted in June 1957, and police were quick to suspect that the same person was responsible for both crimes.

During the investigation that followed, an anonymous letter was received from Norfolk, Virginia, accusing Melvin Rees, a jazz musician, of the crimes, but police searched for Rees without success. The following January the letter-writer contacted them again, this time giving his name as Glenn L. Moser and informing them that Rees was working as a salesman in a music shop in West Memphis, Arkansas. Rees was immediately arrested and identified by a witness to the 1957 murder; a search of his parents' home in Hyattsville resulted in the discovery of the gun used to kill Jackson, together with detailed notes about this and other crimes.

Melvin Rees, a former university student, was known to his friends to be a mild-mannered, intelligent man. He played the piano, the guitar, the saxophone and the clarinet, taking work wherever he could find it. But he had an unusual 'philosophy' of murder: 'You can't say it's wrong to kill,' he had once remarked. 'Only individual standards make it right or wrong.'

Glenn Moser, who knew Rees well, had had cause to ask him outright if he had murdered the Jacksons, and had received an evasive answer. It now became clear that he was a sadist, responsible not only for these and the Annapolis murder, but also for the sex-murders of two teenage girls abducted near the University of Maryland, and two others whose bodies had been recovered from Maryland rivers.

The 'Sex Beast', as he was to be called, was tried for murder, firstly in Maryland, where he was given a life sentence, then in Virginia, where he was sentenced to death. He was executed in 1961, at the age of twenty-eight.

In the Supreme Court of Vancouver, British Columbia, on 12 January 1982, the trial of Clifford Olson, an ex-convict accused of the murder of eleven young people, was brought to a swift conclusion when the defence counsel informed the court that his client, who had earlier denied the offences, wished to change all of his pleas to guilty. When the judge asked the reason for this, he explained that the accused wanted to spare the families of his victims the ordeal of listening to details of the crimes. The pleas were formally registered and a sentence of life imprisonment passed on each charge. The judge recommended that Olson should never be released on parole.

Olson, who was forty-two years old, already had a long record of violent crimes and had, in fact, spent almost all his adult life in jail. Since his release two years earlier, there had been many reports of the disappearance of children and young people in the Vancouver area, and the discovery of three bodies — two boys and a girl — at Weaver Lake, fifty miles east of the city, led to intensive police action.

Olson, living on the outskirts of Vancouver with his wife and baby son, was kept under surveillance. He was arrested in August 1981, after being identified by an eighteen-year-old girl who had been raped while she was out hitch-hiking two months previously. Searching his apartment, police discovered a number of articles belonging to one of the Weaver Lake victims.

Confronted with this evidence, Olson confessed that he was guilty of all three of the murders, and many others, too. He offered to show police where another eight victims had been buried, but only if he was paid $10,000 for each corpse, together with an extra $30,000 for the three which had already been found.

The police refused the offer outright, pointing out that they already had enough evidence to convict him of murder. But, to their astonishment, the Attorney-General, Alan Williams, accepted it, insisting only that $90,000 of the proceeds should be placed in trust for Olson's son. When the money had been paid, and his lawyer was satisfied that it could not be recovered, Olson led police to the sites of eight different graves.

Olson's crimes caused widespread revulsion. His victims, aged between nine and eighteen, had been picked up at random and beaten, stabbed, strangled or mutilated. The revelation, at the end of his trial, that he had been paid $100,000 out of public funds, despite protests from the police, caused much anger. The unprecedented offer was, however, defended by the Solicitor-General, Robert Kaplan, on the grounds that the parents of the victims were entitled to give their children Christian burials.

Two weeks after the payment had been made known to the public, Olson offered the police a 'bargain deal': in return for a further $100,000, he would take them to the graves of twenty other victims. But this time, though he was suspected of many other murders, the offer was not taken up.

A year later, in January 1983, the man who, according to his counsel, had wanted to spare the feelings of his victims' parents, caused further anger by announcing that, in collaboration with a freelance writer, he intended to write a book about his crimes for publication. This led to demands for the law to be changed in order to prevent anyone making a profit out of crime.

Trial of Richard Prince, 1898

At the Old Bailey on 13 January 1898, Richard Prince, an out-of-work actor, was brought to trial for the murder of William Terriss, an immensely popular member of the same profession, at a rear entrance of the Adelphi Theatre, London, on 16 December previously.

Prince, aged thirty-nine, had been born on a farm near Dundee, where his father was a ploughman; his real name was Richard Millar Archer. He was neither a good actor nor a lucky one, and had never been anywhere near the heights to which he aspired; he had made, at best, a meagre living out of occasional small parts.

Of late he had been maintained by payments from the Actors' Benevolent Fund, pawning all but one set of his clothes and existing on meals of bread and milk; his landlady, out of sympathy, had reduced his rent from 4s (20p) to 3s (15p) a week. When his grant was suddenly terminated he became desperate.

He saw Terriss, who had once had him thrown out of a play for making an offensive remark, as the cause of his misfortune. 'He had kept me out of employment for ten years, and I had either to die in the street or kill him,' he was afterwards to declare.

On the evening of his death Terriss, aged fifty, arrived at the theatre where he was appearing in a play called *Secret Service*, in the company of a friend. He intended to enter by a pass-door in Maiden Lane, in order to avoid his fans. But as he inserted his key in the lock, Prince, who had been watching for him, rushed across the street and thrust a kitchen knife into his back with great force.

Terriss turned and fell, a second blow slashing his side and a third inflicting a wound in his chest. He died inside

18

the theatre a little while afterwards. The evening's performance had to be cancelled.

Prince, who had offered no resistance, was handed over to a policeman and taken to Bow Street Police Station. There, having admitted responsibility for the crime, he asked for something to eat. At the committal proceedings the following morning he was subjected to shouts and jeers from the crowds that filled the court.

At his trial Prince wore an Inverness cape. He made a plea of 'guilty with provocation' at first, but changed this on the advice of his counsel to one of not guilty by reason of insanity. Members of his own family and others told the court that his behaviour was unusual, his mother stating that he was 'soft in the head', and medical evidence was given of his 'insane delusions'.

The accused conducted himself throughout in a theatrical manner, as if pleased at having suddenly obtained in real life the leading part which had for so long escaped him on the stage.

The trial lasted one day, the jury deliberating for half an hour before informing the court that they found the accused guilty of the crime but not responsible for his actions. He was committed to the criminal lunatic asylum at Broadmoor and hastily removed from the courtroom after attempting to make a speech of thanks.

He was happier in the asylum than he had been outside and took a keen interest in the entertainments put on by the inmates.

Kidnapping of Lesley Whittle, 1975

On 14 January 1975, Lesley Whittle, aged seventeen, was found to be missing from her home in the village of Highley, in Shropshire. She had not appeared for breakfast that morning and was not in her bedroom. A ransom note, demanding £50,000 for her return, was found on a piece of tape with embossed lettering; it ordered the family not to contact the police and said that a telephone call would be made to a shopping centre in Kidderminster that evening.

Ronald Whittle, the victim's brother, informed the police and later went to the shopping centre to take the call. In the meantime, however, the kidnapping had been reported on television and, as a result, the call was not made.

Two days later, at 11.45 p.m., Ronald Whittle received a telephone call at home, telling him to take the ransom money to a telephone kiosk in Kidsgrove, near Stoke-on-Trent, where he would find another message. He arrived there early in the morning and found the message on a piece of Dynotape, telling him to drive to the nearby Bathpool Park and make contact with the kidnapper by flashing the lights of his car. He followed the instruction, but the kidnapper did not appear.

A further telephone call gave Ronald an opportunity to ask the kidnapper for proof that Lesley was with him. The man agreed to get him the proof — the answer to a certain question — and call back, but he never did so.

By this time the kidnapper was known to have committed other serious crimes. On the night of 15 January a security guard at a transport depot in Dudley, Worcestershire, had seen a shabby little man hanging around the premises and asked him what he wanted. Receiving an

20

unsatisfactory answer, he turned away from the man, intending to call the police, but was shot six times in the back. A stolen car which had been parked nearby was found to contain Lesley's slippers, more messages from the kidnapper, and a tape-recording made by Lesley asking her family to co-operate with him.

Moreover, an examination of the cartridge cases found at the depot showed that the same gun had been used by a notorious criminal called the 'Black Panther', who specialized in sub-post office burglaries and was known to have committed three murders.

An intensive police search led to the discovery, on 7 March 1975, of Lesley Whittle's body in the network of sewage tunnels underneath Bathpool Park; it was hanging, naked, by a wire rope below a narrow ledge. The sewage system had been the kidnapper's hide-out and his victim's place of captivity.

On 11 December the same year two policemen driving through Mansfield Woodhouse, Nottinghamshire, late at night noticed a suspicious-looking man loitering near the post office and stopped to speak to him. The man produced a sawn-off shotgun and ordered them to drive him to Blidworth, six miles away. But they managed, with the help of two members of the public, to overpower him, and found in his possession two hoods of the sort known to have been used by the Black Panther.

The man turned out to be Donald Neilson, aged thirty-nine, of Grangefield Avenue, Thornaby, Bradford, a married man with a teenage daughter. Neilson, who had changed his name from Nappey, was a joiner and occasional taxi-driver. But in his attic police found more guns and hoods, together with burglary equipment.

Neilson was tried in Oxford in June 1976 for the kidnapping and murder of Lesley Whittle, for which he was sentenced to twenty-one years' imprisonment. He was then tried for the murders of three sub-postmasters and sentenced to life imprisonment for each offence. No charge was brought against him in connection with the shooting of the security guard in Dudley, as the victim in this case had lived for fourteen months after the offence had been committed.

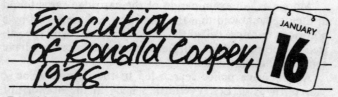

Execution of Ronald Cooper, 1978

Ronald Frank Cooper, who was hanged in South Africa on 16 January 1978, was a fantasist who wanted to become a mass murderer. Fortunately for the rest of society, he was assailed by doubt and misfortune in his attempts to put his ideas into practice.

Cooper had a troubled childhood: he is known to have hated his father and to have tried, at the age of eleven, to strangle a girl. Early in 1976 he was an unemployed labourer living in a hotel in Berea, Johannesburg. It was then that he committed his first-known crime as an adult.

Following a ten-year-old boy into an apartment block in a different district of Johannesburg, he pulled out a gun and forced the child to accompany him to a nearby park. There, however, he suddenly gave up whatever he had in mind and allowed his victim to go home. The boy, Tresslin Pohl, was later taken out in a police car to look for him, but without success.

A month later, on 17 March 1976, Ronald Cooper made a long entry in his diary, no doubt to convince himself that he was now more resolute than he had been before. He began, falteringly enough: 'I have decided that I think I should become a homosexual murderer ...' Then, taking the bull by the horns, he continued: '... and shall get hold of young boys and bring them here where I am staying and I shall rape them and then kill them.'

22

Soon his imagination was running wild: 'I shall not kill all the boys in the same way. Some I shall strangle with my hands. Other boys I shall strangle with a piece of cord or rope. Others again I shall stab to death, and others I shall cut their throats. I can also suffocate or smother other boys ...'

He went on and on, listing different ways in which he would dispose of his victims, finally stating that after killing thirty boys, he would turn his attention to the opposite sex and kill at least six girls or women. Yet, in spite of this, he remained as half-hearted as ever in practice.

Four days after making this entry Cooper followed another ten-year-old boy into a block of flats. Pushing him against a wall, he pressed a knife against his chest, inflicting two minor wounds, but ran off when the boy screamed. At his next attempt, in a block in his own district, he pulled a boy out of the lift and tried to strangle him, but once again took to his heels when the victim screamed.

On 16 May, in yet another apartment block, he grasped Mark Garnet, aged twelve, by the throat. When the boy lost consciousness Cooper tied a rope round his neck and made an unsuccessful attempt at sodomy. Afterwards he loosened the rope, hoping that the boy was still alive. But this time the attack had been fatal.

Overcome with remorse, Cooper described the murder in three different diaries — a clear sign of mental conflict. 'I only wish I can undo what I did,' he wrote in one of them. 'It's a really dreadful thing that I did. I never want to do such a thing again.'

He was not to have any more opportunities, for Tresslin Pohl, a schoolfriend of Mark Garnet's, had discovered where Cooper was living: he had followed him home after seeing him in a cinema and, surprisingly, kept this information to himself. But now, hearing of Mark's death, he decided to go to the police.

Police officers went immediately to the hotel and waited in a car near the entrance. When Cooper emerged he took fright at the sight of them, and after a brief chase, was taken into custody. The diaries found in his room left no doubt about his guilt.

Cooper was twenty-six years old at the time of his execution.

Execution of Gary Gilmore, 1977

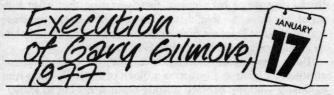

JANUARY 17

On 17 January 1977, Gary Gilmore, a double murderer, was executed by firing squad in the State of Utah, at his own insistence. It was the outcome of a successful legal battle over what he called 'the right to die' and brought an end to a ten-year moratorium on the death penalty in the United States. The case was, of course, highly publicized and provided Norman Mailer with a subject for a very successful book, *The Executioner's Song.*

Nine months earlier Gilmore, aged thirty-five, had been released on parole from the federal penitentiary in Marion, Illinois, after serving over eleven years. A violent and dangerous man, he had, in fact, spent more than half of his life in detention, and during his last term, he and a friend had beaten and knifed a fellow-convict so badly that he had almost died.

He had, it seems, no intention of making good. He drank heavily and began stealing from stores, the thefts being the result of habit rather than need. The two murders were committed in July 1976, robbery being the motive in each case.

The first murder was that of Max Jensen, a law student working at a service station in Orem, Utah; Gilmore held him up, forced him into the men's room, and shot him in the back of the head while he lay on the floor The second

24

which took place the following evening, was that of Ben Bushnell, the manager of the City Centre Motel in Provo, a few miles away; the victim was shot dead in the same way. In each case Gilmore stole about $125 in cash.

On the latter occasion he was seen by the victim's wife and a guest at the motel. Afterwards, in disposing of the gun, he accidentally shot himself in the hand. The wound was noticed at a nearby garage when he went to collect his truck, which had been left for servicing, and was later reported to the police. Gilmore was arrested without difficulty while trying to leave the state by road.

His determination to avoid a commutation of sentence was due not to remorse, but to a fear of further long-term imprisonment. He told his brother, who intended to apply for a stay of execution on his behalf: 'I've spent too much time in jail. I don't have anything left in me.'

At one point he persuaded a girl with whom he was in love to smuggle drugs in to him, so that they could both commit suicide at a pre-arranged time. But the attempt failed and the girl was removed to a mental hospital for treatment.

As a result of his demand to be executed, Gilmore became a celebrity, selling the rights to his life story for about $50,000. On the night before his death he gave a farewell party inside the prison for his relatives and friends. Early the following morning he instructed his lawyers to appeal against a last-minute stay of execution; they did so, and the order was set aside.

The execution was carried out in a local cannery to which Gilmore had been taken by van. He was strapped down in an old office chair, with a dirty mattress behind the backboard to prevent ricochets. A light was shone on to him, while everyone else was in semi-darkness. When a hood had been pulled over his face, the members of the firing squad took aim from behind a screen, training their guns on a white ring pinned above his heart.

Murder of Julia Wallace, 1931

On the evening of 20 January 1931, Julia Wallace, the fifty-year-old wife of an insurance agent, was found battered to death in the sitting-room of her home in Wolverton Street, Liverpool. She had been struck over the head eleven times — many of the blows being dealt when she was already dead — and the walls, furniture and carpet of the room were drenched with blood. An iron bar which the couple had kept for cleaning the fireplace was missing from the house, and it appeared that about £4 in cash had also been taken. The iron bar, which was never found, was almost certainly the murder weapon.

Her husband, William Herbert Wallace, aged fifty-two, informed the police that a telephone message had been left for him at his chess club the previous evening by an unknown man calling himself Qualtrough. The message was that Qualtrough wanted to speak to him on a matter of business and that the insurance agent should call at his home in Menlove Gardens East, Mossley Hill, at 7.30 p.m. the following day. Wallace had accordingly left his own home about 6.50 p.m. and travelled by tramcar to the Menlove Gardens area of Liverpool, only to discover that Menlove Gardens East did not exist.

Arriving back at his own home about 8.45 p.m., Wallace had called for assistance from his neighbours, Mr and Mrs Johnston, saying that he was unable to get into his house because the doors wouldn't open. But when they went to help him they found that his back door, at least, opened without difficulty. The body was discovered a moment later, Wallace being strangely calm at the sight of it.

The police were suspicious of Wallace's account of his movements, especially as they could find no sign of a forced entry. It also seemed, from the pathologist's report, that Mrs Wallace had been killed before her husband left the house that evening. As for the telephone call to his chess club, that was found to have been made from a telephone box less than a quarter of a mile from Wolverton Street. So Wallace could easily have made it himself.

After continuing their investigation for two weeks, the police arrested Wallace and charged him with the crime. He was brought to trial at St George's Hall, Liverpool, on 22 April. But the case proved not to be very strong, and the judge, in his summing-up, suggested to the jury that it was insufficient to justify a conviction.

Wallace had had no motive for killing his wife. They had been a devoted couple, leading conventional lives, and he had stood to gain nothing from her death. Mrs Wallace, according to the evidence of a milk delivery boy, had still been alive at 6.30 that evening; her husband had boarded a tramcar at Smithdown Junction, a ten-minute walk from the house, at 7.10. Later, when the murder was reported, no bloodstains had been found on any of his clothes, except a macintosh on which his dead wife's body had actually been lying.

Yet, incredibly, the jury disregarded the judge's advice and returned a verdict of guilty. Wallace, under sentence of death, appealed against the conviction, and won his case before the Court of Criminal Appeal. He died two years later, claiming to the end that he knew the real identity of his wife's murderer.

The case is still the subject of much speculation.

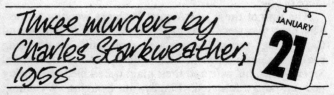

Three murders by Charles Starkweather, 1958

JANUARY
21

On 21 January 1958, Charles Starkweather, a nineteen-year-old garbage collector of Lincoln, Nebraska, called at

27

the home of his girlfriend, Caril Ann Fugate, aged fourteen. She was not there at the time, so her mother and stepfather, Velda and Marion Bartlett, allowed him into the house to await her return. He was carrying a hunting rifle, and began to play with it while he was waiting.

Being only 5 feet 2 inches tall, and having red hair, Starkweather was known as 'Little Red'. He drove a hot-rod and read comics; the film star James Dean was his personal hero. But his girlfriend's mother was evidently uneasy in his presence, for she shouted at him, telling him to stop fiddling with his gun. At this, Starkweather shot both Mrs Bartlett and her husband dead. He then went on waiting until Caril returned.

Caril Fugate knew what Starkweather was like, for a few weeks earlier she had joined him in carrying out a robbery at a gas station, during the course of which the attendant had been murdered. She was not distressed when she arrived home and found that he had killed her mother and stepfather, and apparently raised no objection when he went into one of the bedrooms and choked her two-year-old stepsister to death. The couple calmly put a notice on the front door, stating: 'Every Body is Sick with the Flu'. They then made some sandwiches and sat down to watch television, as if oblivious of the corpses lying around.

A few days later the two teenagers drove off in Stark-weather's hot-rod, making their way across America. The police broke into the house in Lincoln and raised an alert, but it was several days before the couple were arrested and during that time the former garbage collector killed seven more people.

The first of these was August Meyer, a wealthy farmer. The next two were a teenage couple, Robert Jensen and Carol King; the girl was raped repeatedly before being beaten to death. Then C. Lauer Ward, head of the Capital Steel Works, his wife and their maid were killed after being tied up and mutilated. Finally, in Douglas, Wyoming, Merle Collison, a shoe salesman, was shot dead.

Attempting to get away from the scene of this last

crime, Starkweather found that his car would not start, and tried to force a passer-by to help him. The passer-by, an oil agent named Joseph Sprinkle, grabbed his rifle and held on to it until the police arrived. There were, by this time, 1200 police and members of the National Guard in pursuit of the couple, and they were quickly arrested, Starkweather surrendering after being grazed by a bullet.

Starkweather at first tried to protect the girl by telling the police that he had taken her hostage, but he stopped doing so when she called him a killer. He made a confession, declaring his hatred of the society he knew, which seemed to him to be made up entirely of 'Goddam sons of bitches looking for somebody to make fun of'. He was executed in the electric chair at the Nebraska State Penitentiary on 25 June 1959.

Caril Fugate, who claimed to be innocent of the crimes to which Starkweather had confessed, was sentenced to life imprisonment. She was released on parole in 1977.

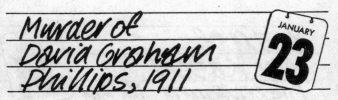

Murder of David Graham Phillips, 1911

JANUARY 23

The murder of David Graham Phillips, on 23 January 1911, was a ludicrous crime, committed as a result of a false assumption on the part of his killer, Fitzhugh Coyle Goldsborough, who killed himself immediately afterwards.

Phillips, aged forty-three, was a popular author whose novel, *The Fashionable Adventures of Joshua Craig*, was among the best-sellers of the time. He had an apartment in Gramercy Park, Manhattan.

Goldsborough, aged thirty, was a member of a rich Philadelphia family. He had no occupation and no apparent aim; much of his time was spent lying in bed, either reading love stories or turning neurotic ideas over in his mind. He did not know Phillips personally.

Somehow, Goldsborough had conceived the notion that his unmarried sister, whom he adored, had been used as a real-life model for a flippant society girl in Phillips' novel, and this he regarded as a slight which had to be avenged.

The murder took place just after Phillips left his apartment on the day in question. Goldsborough, according to witnesses, confronted him with a pistol, shouting, 'Here you go!' He then shot Phillips five times before turning the gun on himself. As he fired his last shot he screamed, 'Here I go!'

Phillips was taken to hospital, where he lived for some hours. As he died he remarked, 'I can fight one bullet, but not five.'

When Goldsborough's parents were told what had happened they revealed the reason for his astonishing conduct.

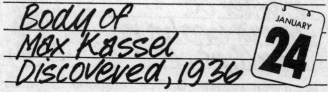

Body of Max Kassel Discovered, 1936

JANUARY 24

About ten o'clock on the morning of 24 January 1936, a man's body was discovered in a country lane near St Albans, Hertfordshire. He had died from gunshot wounds a few hours earlier, having been beaten up beforehand. There was nothing in his pockets to reveal his identity, and all marks had been removed from his clothes. It was speculated in the press that he had been the victim of a gang killing.

Three days later he was identified as Émile Allard, a

dealer in cheap jewellery. Émile Allard, however, turned out to be one of many aliases of an international crook named Max Kassel, generally known as 'Red Max'.

Kassel was a Latvian, born in 1879. He had a criminal record in France, where he had been imprisoned in 1922 for drug-trafficking, and was also known to have been involved in a vice racket in South America. More recently he had lived in Soho, arranging marriages — or, at least, marriage ceremonies — for Frenchwomen who wanted to obtain British nationality. He had been seen in Soho about 7.30 p.m. on 23 January.

During the course of their inquiries police officers learnt that Kassel had been accustomed to using the car-hire services of a Frenchman named Alexandre, who, on being interviewed, gave the impression of knowing more about the affair than he was willing to divulge.

Investigating his background, they found that he held the lease of a two-floor flat in Little Newport Street, occupied by Suzanne Naylor, a Frenchwoman married to an Englishman. Mrs Naylor was known to have a lover named Georges Lacroix, who normally lived with her at the Little Newport Street address. But neither of them were to be found there when the police went to see them.

Suspicious, the police broke in and searched the place, finding some broken window-panes and specks of blood in the bathroom. But there were no fingerprints anywhere and no clothes in the cupboards. The couple had cleaned the flat as thoroughly as possible and fled.

From a Ministry of Health insurance card, found behind a chest of drawers, the police traced a second French-woman, Marcelle Aubin, who had been employed as Suzanne Naylor's maid. Marcelle Aubin informed them that her employer had left for France on 25 January.

Alexandre was questioned further and obliged to surrender his American car for examination. When blood-stains were found in it he decided to tell the police what had happened.

He said that Lacroix had telephoned him late at night

31

on 23 January and told him to go to the flat in Little Newport Street. When he arrived there he was shown Kassel's body and told to return at 4 a.m. to help dispose of it, Lacroix threatening him with a gun. At 4 a.m. he and Lacroix had taken the body, wrapped in a blanket, out to his car. They had then driven to St Albans together.

Kassel, he explained, had owed Suzanne Naylor £25. Lacroix had started to beat him up because he had failed to pay it back, and had shot him when Kassel resisted. The victim had broken the window in an attempt to call for help.

This account was confirmed by Marcelle Aubin, who now admitted that she had been present and that she had heard the fighting, the shots and a constant groaning from another room. She had stayed in the flat all night, helping Suzanne to remove traces of the crime, she said.

Suzanne Naylor was located in France, where she was known to the police as Paulette Bernard. She had been legally married in France before coming to England, and so was still a French citizen. Georges Lacroix proved to be an alias of Robert Vernon, a Frenchman with a record of larceny with violence, who had escaped from Devil's Island in 1927.

As extradition was impossible, it was arranged that they would both be tried in Paris, Vernon for murder and his mistress for being an accessory after the fact. Chief Inspector F.D. Sharpe of the Flying Squad had therefore to give evidence against them before a French court.

In April 1937 Robert Vernon was convicted of the murder and sentenced to ten years' hard labour and twenty years' banishment to French Guiana. Paulette Bernard, who claimed to have been an unwilling participant, was acquitted.

Mass Poisoning in Tokyo, 1948

JANUARY
26

Just before closing time on 26 January 1948, a man entered a branch of the Imperial Bank in north Tokyo, claiming to be one of the city's public health officials. Announcing that there had been an outbreak of dysentery in the area, he induced all sixteen of the bank's employees to drink a solution of potassium cyanide. He then proceeded to rob the tills as his victims collapsed around him, and made off with a large amount of money in cash and cheques. Only four members of the staff survived.

Seven months later Sadamichi Hirasawa, a fifty-six-year-old artist of Otaru, Hokkaido, was arrested in connection with the murders. Normally a poor man, Hirasawa was unable to explain a comparatively large sum of money found in his possession, and eventually confessed to the crime. He afterwards retracted the confession, saying that it had been obtained after thirty-seven days of intensive questioning, but he was convicted and sentenced to death.

The sentence was confirmed in 1955 but never carried out, as successive Justice Ministers, for some undisclosed reason, refused to give their approval to the execution order. Sadamichi Hirasawa has remained in prison ever since and his sentence has never been commuted. He is said to have been on Death Row longer than anyone else in the world.

But many doubts have been expressed about his guilt, and there have been many demands for a retrial. Of the four surviving members of the bank staff, three said only that he bore a resemblance to the person responsible for the crime, while the fourth could see no resemblance at all. Moreover, it is now known that the Japanese police did not believe him to be guilty, either.

33

Following his retirement in 1963, Hideo Noruchi, the police officer in charge of the investigation, revealed that his team of detectives had believed the culprit to be experienced in the use of poisons, and had suspected a member of the 731st Regiment of the Imperial Japanese Army. This regiment had been involved in chemical warfare research during the Second World War, using Chinese prisoners in its experiments. But its war record had been ignored by General MacArthur's Occupation Force in return for the information which had been gained.

It appears from contemporary documents which have recently been discovered in the United States that MacArthur's General Headquarters also believed the poisoner to have been a member of the 731st Regiment, but forced the Japanese police to frame an innocent man rather than allow the connection to be exposed. Japanese newspapers which tried to investigate the case at the time were censored — also on orders from MacArthur's GHQ. And an American soldier with whom Hirasawa claimed to have been playing cards on the afternoon in question was recalled from Japan before the trial started in 1949.

In February 1984 Hirasawa, then aged ninety-two, was reported to be confined to bed and going blind in Sendai Jail. A plea for clemency was made on his behalf by a group of supporters called the Save Hirasawa Committee, whose members include Takeshiko Hirasawa, the artist's adopted son. The plea was unsuccessful.

In May 1985 an attempt was made to get him released under Japan's Statute of Limitations, as thirty years had elapsed since his death sentence had been confirmed. But this also failed because the thirty-year rule was interpreted as applying only to accused persons who had not been captured or who had escaped from custody.

It seems likely that the fight to clear Hirasawa's name will continue long after his death.

Murder of Frieda Rösner, 1943

On 29 January 1943, a woman's body was found in a wood near the village of Köpenick, near Berlin. Frieda Rösner, aged fifty-one, had been out collecting firewood; her death was caused by strangulation. There were no obvious suspects, so the police officer in charge of the case began questioning known criminals from the village. One of these was Bruno Lüdke, a laundry roundsman who had earlier been sterilized after being arrested for sexual assault.

Lüdke, who was mentally defective, admitted that he had known the victim and that he had seen her in the woods. On being asked if he had killed her, he became violent and had to be restrained. He then admitted the crime and went on to confess that he was guilty of eighty-four other murders in different parts of Germany. Some of these murders were found to be on record as unsolved crimes; others were found to be offences for which innocent men had been arrested. At any rate, after an investigation lasting a year, it was concluded that Lüdke's confession was true.

Born in 1909, Lüdke had committed his first murder in 1928. His victims had all been women, rape being his usual motive, although he also robbed them; their deaths were normally caused either by strangulation or by stabbing. On another occasion he had derived pleasure from running a woman down with his horse-drawn delivery van. In addition to all this, he had been in the habit of torturing animals.

Instead of being brought to trial, Lüdke was removed to a hospital in Vienna, where he was used for experiments. He was finally put to death by means of an injection on 8 April 1944.

The Nazis treated the case as a state secret.

Execution of Kenneth Neu, 1935

Kenneth Neu, who was hanged in New Orleans on 1 February 1935, was an aspiring night-club singer with a record of mental illness. On 2 September 1933, while he was out of work in New York, he met Lawrence Shead, a homosexual theatre-owner. Shead took him for a drink, offered him a job, and invited him back to his apartment. There, however, it became clear that his real interest in him was a sexual one. Neu smashed in Shead's skull with an electric iron, put on one of his suits, and made off with his watch and wallet.

Two weeks later, in New Orleans, he met Eunice Hotter, a young waitress with whom he spent the next three nights. Eunice wanted to go to New York and Neu promised to take her there, but by now he was out of money again and decided to try blackmail.

In the lobby of the Jung Hotel, he became acquainted with Sheffield Clark, a Nashville store-owner aged sixty-three. Calling on Clark later in his room, he demanded money from him, threatening to accuse him of making homosexual advances. When Clark reached for the telephone to call the police, Neu hit him with a blackjack and strangled him. He took $300 and Clark's car keys and went to the car park to get his car, telling the attendant that he was the owner's son. He then set out for New York with Eunice Hotter, having first replaced the number plate of the stolen car with a notice chalked on a piece of cardboard: 'New Car in Transit'.

Driving through New Jersey, he was stopped by the police, who asked what the notice meant. Unable to give a satisfactory explanation, he spent the night in jail — as did Eunice Hotter and a hitch-hiker who had been in the car with them. It was then noticed that he fitted the description of a man wanted in connection with Shead's murder.

Asked if he knew Shead, Neu replied, 'Sure ... I killed him. This is his suit I'm wearing now.' He went on to confess that he had also killed Sheffield Clark. 'He seemed like a nice old man,' he said. 'But I was desperate for money.' In view of Shead's homosexuality, it was decided that Neu should be sent back to New Orleans to be tried for Clark's murder.

Neu, aged twenty-five, was a handsome man with an engaging manner. It was partly because of this that his trial, which opened on 12 December 1933, attracted a lot of attention. He appeared in court wearing Shead's suit and pleaded insanity, evidence being given that he had suffered mental deterioration as a result of syphilis. As if to emphasize the point, Neu sang on his way to and from the courtroom. He was, however, convicted, and an appeal was turned down.

On Death Row he remained cheerful, singing and tap-dancing in his cell, and receiving visits from a young woman who had apparently fallen in love with him. At the gallows he sang a verse which he had composed himself, beginning, 'I'm fit as a fiddle and ready to hang'.

While under sentence of death he had also become a Roman Catholic.

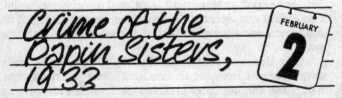

Crime of the Papin Sisters, 1933

FEBRUARY 2

On the evening of 2 February 1933, René Lancelin, a French attorney living in Le Mans, arrived for dinner at the home of a friend. He had been away all day on business and expected that his wife and twenty-seven-year-old daughter Geneviève, who had also been invited, would meet him there. But they had not turned up and his friend had had no word from them.

M. Lancelin waited for a little while, then tried to telephone his home. He received no reply. Becoming worried, he excused himself and went to find out what had happened. He found his own house in darkness, except for a faint glow from an upstairs room occupied by their maids, the sisters Christine and Lea Papin. Moreover, he was unable to get into the house as the front door had been locked from the inside. He therefore called the police.

An inspector came to his assistance, forcing his way into the house. He found the ground floor to be deserted. But on the first floor landing lay the bodies of the attorney's wife and daughter, revoltingly mutilated: the walls and doors had been splashed with blood to a height of over seven feet. The police officer immediately went in search of the maids and, finding their room locked, broke down the door. Inside, the two women lay huddled together, naked, in a bed.

They both confessed to the crime, which appeared to have been committed because Madame Lancelin had rebuked them over a blown fuse. 'When I saw that Madame Lancelin was going to jump on me I leapt at her face and scratched out her eyes with my fingers,' said Christine Papin. She then realized that she had made a mistake and quickly corrected herself: 'No ... it was on Mademoiselle Lancelin that I leapt, and it was her eyes that I scratched out. Meanwhile, my sister Lea had jumped on Madame Lancelin and scratched her eyes out in the same way.'

After this, she continued, she had brought up a knife and a hammer from the kitchen, and with these two instruments she and her sister attacked their victims afresh. 'We struck at the head with the knife, hacked at the bodies and legs, and also struck with a pewter pot, which was standing on a little table on the landing. We exchanged one instrument for another several times. By that I mean that I would pass the hammer over to my sister so that she could hit with it, while she handed me the knife — and we did the same with the pewter pot.'

She said that she had locked the attorney out because she wanted the police to be the first to arrive on the scene, and that they had taken their clothes off because they were stained with blood. 'I have no regrets — or, rather, I can't tell you whether I have any or not ... I did not plan my crime and I didn't feel any hatred towards them (the victims), but I don't put up with the sort of gesture that Madame Lancelin was making at me that evening.'

Lea corroborated Christine's account. 'Like my sister, I affirm that we had not planned to kill our mistresses,' she said. 'The idea came suddenly, when we heard Madame Lancelin scolding us.'

Christine Papin, aged twenty-eight, and her sister Lea, twenty-one, were brought to trial in Le Mans in September 1933. They were already regarded as notorious criminals by this time, and the newspapers referred to them as 'the diabolical sisters', and 'the lambs who had become wolves'. As the details of their crime were given in the courtroom, there were murmurs of horror and demands for their execution from the spectators. The prisoners listened impassively.

The judge questioned them about their motive, finding it impossible to believe that they could have made such ferocious attacks on their victims just because they were being scolded over a blown fuse. They had, after all, both agreed that they had been well paid and well treated by the family, and bore no resentment as a result of being their servants.

Observing that the prisoners had led unusually isolated lives for young people, with no social activities and no contact with members of the opposite sex, the judge asked whether they had had a sexual relationship with each other. But Christine replied, with a shrug, that they were just sisters; there was nothing else between them.

As no satisfactory explanation of the crime emerged, the defence naturally pleaded that the prisoners were not of sound mind. The jury, however, returned verdicts of guilty against both of them, though with extenuating circumstances in Lea's case, as she had been dominated by Christine. The judge then sentenced Christine to death and Lea to ten years' hard labour.

Christine's sentence was afterwards commuted to hard labour for life, but she began to show signs of insanity not long afterwards and died in a psychiatric hospital in 1937. Lea was released after serving her term.

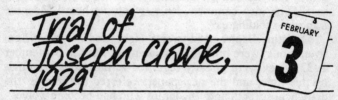

Trial of Joseph Clark, 1929

FEBRUARY 3

On 3 February 1929, Joseph Clark, aged twenty-one, was brought to trial at the Liverpool Assize Court, charged with the murder of Alice Fontaine, his former landlady. He pleaded guilty, against the advice of his counsel, and was sentenced to death. It was one of the shortest murder trials on record, lasting just four and a half minutes. He was afterwards hanged.

Clark was an amateur hypnotist who lived off his many girlfriends. He had been brought up by relatives in the United States, but worked his passage back to England in 1927. He seems to have had little difficulty inducing girls to part with their money; one of them said later, 'I could not resist him, and would do anything he suggested ... I gave him money whenever he wanted it ...'

In Birkenhead he tried to marry a girl who was under twenty-one by presenting her older sister's birth certificate at the registrar's office. When the attempt was discovered he became enraged and tried to strangle the girl with a pyjama cord, shouting, 'If I can't have you nobody else shall!' No charge was brought against him over this, as the girl was afraid of the publicity which would result from it.

Clark became a lodger at Mrs Fontaine's house in Northbrook Street, Liverpool, after meeting her daughter whose name was also Alice; he was now calling himself Kennedy. He failed to pay for his keep and constantly borrowed money. When he was finally turned out — after the discovery of a letter from one of his other victims — he sent obscene letters to both mother and daughter.

Shortly afterwards, in October 1928, Clark suddenly appeared in the daughter's bedroom as she was getting ready to go to church. He tried to strangle her, again using a pyjama cord, and after a struggle she lost consciousness. She recovered a little later and found that he had also attempted to cut her throat. Her mother's body was found downstairs, Clark's attempt to strangle Mrs Fontaine having been more successful.

After being arrested Clark made a confession. He claimed that in her last moments, after he had relaxed his grip on her throat, Mrs Fontaine had smiled at him and asked him to take care of her daughter.

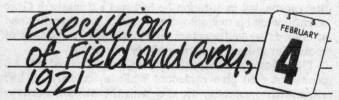

Execution of Field and Gray, 1921

FEBRUARY 4

On 4 February 1921, Jack Alfred Field, aged nineteen, and William Thomas Gray, twenty-nine, were hanged at Wandsworth Prison for a brutal murder committed on a stretch of shingle near Eastbourne on 19 August the previous year.

Their victim, Irene Munro, a Scottish-born typist from London, was seventeen years old. She had been spending a week's holiday at an Eastbourne boarding-house, and on the afternoon of the day in question was known to have been carrying her holiday money in her handbag.

A number of people noticed her in the company of two men, one of whom wore a herring-bone suit. Her body was afterwards found in a shallow grave; she had been battered to death with a stone, and her money had been stolen. It was the landlady of the boarding-house who identified the body.

Field and Gray were local residents, both out of work. They were initially questioned by police as a result of Gray's herring-bone suit, but were not regarded as suspects at this stage. Later, however, it was learnt from a barmaid at the Albemarle Hotel that they had been out of money on the morning of 19 August, but apparently affluent a few hours afterwards.

Then, during a house-to-house inquiry, a labourer stated that he had seen Gray, whom he knew personally, walking towards the shingle that afternoon with another man and a girl. The two culprits were arrested and charged with the crime.

They appeared for trial at the Lewes Assizes on 13 December 1920, denying the offence. Though witnesses had seen them in the girl's company, Field told the court that on the day in question he had had a drink with Gray after drawing his unemployment benefit, and that they had afterwards walked together to Pevensey — a distance of about four miles — meeting nobody on the way.

Gray, an unsavoury character, was advised by his counsel not to give evidence. While in custody he had attempted to establish an alibi with the help of a fellow-prisoner; during the course of the trial he fell asleep and was rebuked by the judge. His counsel suggested to the jury that an educated and refined girl like Irene Munro was unlikely to have associated with down-and-out men like the prisoners.

While under sentence of death the two ruffians both accused each other of the girl's murder. We do not know which of them was telling the truth.

Bodies of Ted Williams' daughters discovered, 1924

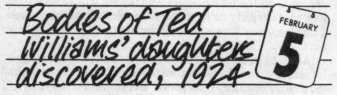

On the morning of 5 February 1924, Edward Williams, a poor music teacher living in a suburb of Sydney, was returning from Mass when he stopped to speak to a crossing-sweeper named Tonkin, and offered to buy him a drink. Tonkin was surprised, for Williams did not normally drink and was known to be having a very hard time. However, he went with him to a working-men's bar where the music teacher ordered two glasses of stout.

During the course of their conversation Williams said that he was taking his three daughters to Brisbane, where he had been offered a position as choirmaster. Tonkin, he said, could have his furniture in settlement of a debt; he could go and collect it from his lodgings. The crossing-sweeper was impressed and gave Williams enough money to get the four of them to Brisbane. Later, after parting company with him, he took a handcart to the music teacher's lodgings to move the furniture.

His arrival threw Williams' landlady, Florence Mahon, into a state of confusion. She rushed upstairs to Williams' room, to see what he had to say about it. But Williams wasn't there. Instead, she found his three little girls lying together in bed, all with their throats cut. Their blood had soaked through the mattress on to some newspaper which had been spread underneath it.

The police started a search for Williams, but he was

nowhere to be found. He was still at large when the bodies of the children were buried.

Among those who knew him, the crime caused dismay as well as horror, for Ted Williams had loved his children: they had been a source of great pleasure to him, in spite of his otherwise troubled existence. A neighbour who had seen him on the afternoon of 4 February was to recall: 'He looked extremely tired until he smiled at his daughters. Then his whole face lit up and the tiredness seemed to leave him.'

After being on the run for several days Williams gave himself up and made a confession. He said that he had killed his daughters because he was frightened for them. 'I knew what I was doing,' he said. 'I was doing it for the best, because I loved them.' He was charged with murder.

Ted Williams, aged fifty-two, was a man prone to misfortune. His income had never been high and he had always found it difficult to make ends meet. For the last two years his wife, Florence Mahon's sister-in-law, had been confined in an asylum, and he and his three daughters, the eldest of whom was five and a half, had lived and slept in one room. While he went hungry to ensure that they had an adequate amount of food, he was treated with contempt by his brother-in-law who regarded him as 'a bum'. By 4 February he was close to the end of his tether.

On that day, Florence Mahon, who looked after the children for him while he went out to give lessons, said that she would do it no more: he would have to find somebody else. Later the same day her husband suggested that he should send them to an institution because they were now too old to sleep in the same room as him.

To Ted Williams, Mahon's remark was a shattering blow. When he came up for trial at the Central Court in Sydney, he told the jury: 'I saw if my girls went to an institution they would be separated. They would not be able to sit at the same table together, and when they came out they would be tools for the first smooth-tongued person who came along. I know — and you know, gentlemen — that

44

the majority of prostitutes are the women who were raised in public institutions such as my girls would have been sent to had I been agreeable. I saw it all, and saw beyond it.' Rather than allow that to happen, he had murdered them in their sleep.

He denied that he was insane; he denied that he had tried to escape justice. 'I intended to give myself up, but decided not to do so until the Monday, in order that I might learn that my children were properly buried,' he explained.

Ted Williams was convicted and sentenced to death. Many thousands of letters were sent to the Minister of Justice, Thomas Ley, asking for the sentence to be commuted. But they were brushed aside, the execution being carried out at Long Bay Jail.

Thomas Ley was later convicted of murder himself and died in Broadmoor. An account of his crime also appears in this book (see 30 November).

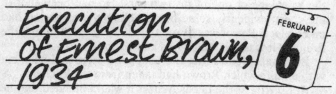

Execution of Ernest Brown, 1934

FEBRUARY 6

Ernest Brown, who was hanged on 6 February 1934, at the age of thirty-five, had been employed as a groom by Frederick Morton, a wealthy cattle-dealer of Saxton Grange, an isolated farmhouse near the village of Towton, in Yorkshire. While working in that capacity he had been having an affair with Dorothy Morton, the cattle-dealer's wife. But he proved to be a possessive man with a violent temper, and Mrs Morton found this irksome.

In June 1933 he became indignant at being asked to mow the lawn, which he did not consider to be one of his duties; he promptly left Morton's employment. A little while afterwards he sought, with Mrs Morton's help, to get the job back, but found that his former employer would now only accept him as an odd-job man. Brown therefore returned to Saxton Grange seething with resentment and promising himself revenge.

On the evening of 5 September, while his employer was away, he started an argument with Dorothy Morton because she had been out swimming with another man; he struck her and she fell to the ground. The same evening the telephone was found to be out of order and Brown began firing a shotgun outside the house, saying that he was shooting at rats. Dorothy Morton became frightened, having only her baby and her young help, Ann Houseman, for company, and soon the two women took the child and locked themselves in upstairs rooms.

At 3.30 a.m. there was an explosion outside and they saw that the garage was on fire. They left the house in terror, running into the nearby fields. In the morning the ruins of the garage, which had been completely destroyed, were examined, and the cattle-dealer's body was found in the wreckage of one of his two cars. He had been shot in the chest, evidently some hours before the explosion had taken place. Petrol was found to have been used to fuel the fire, and it was this which had caused the explosion.

It was also found that the telephone wires had been cut with a knife which Brown had taken from the kitchen.

At his trial at the Leeds Assizes it was contended that he had cut the wires after killing Frederick Morton about 9.30 p.m., and then frightened the women to prevent them leaving the house. His own claim, that Morton had caused the fire himself as a result of being drunk, was not taken seriously.

Ernest Brown's execution took place at Armley Prison in Leeds. While on the scaffold he was asked by the chaplain if he wanted to confess any other crimes before being hanged. His reply, 'Ought to burn!' or 'Otterburn!' has given rise to the idea that he may have been the murderer of Evelyn Foster. Unfortunately, the trap opened before he could make himself clear on this point.

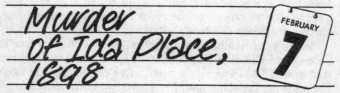

Murder of Ida Place, 1898

Just after 6.30 p.m. on 7 February 1898, a New York City policeman arrived at the Brooklyn home of William Place, a prosperous forty-seven-year-old insurance adjuster, accompanied by a neighbour who had reported hearing screams and cries for help from inside. He rang the bell and waited for a moment, then, hearing a moan himself, got the neighbour to help him force an entry.

Inside the house, a few feet from the front door, the two men found Place lying unconscious on the floor. He had serious head injuries and his face was smeared with blood. There was a smell of gas about the place.

Sending the neighbour to summon an ambulance, the patrolman tended the injured man. The precinct commander and two detectives arrived soon afterwards and began to search the premises, leaving Place in the hands of the ambulance crew. There appeared at first to be nobody else in the house, but tracing the smell of gas to one of the front bedrooms, the police officers found Place's wife Martha, also unconscious, wrapped in a quilt on the floor. She too, was taken to hospital, to be treated for gas poisoning.

But with the windows open and the gas cleared, another smell — that of carbolic acid — caused the police to force open the locked door of one of the other bedrooms. There, under the mattress of a disordered bed, they found the body of Place's daughter Ida, aged seventeen.

Ida Place had been dead for several hours. Her face had

been disfigured with acid burns while she was still alive; she had also received a heavy blow on the left temple. But her death had been caused by strangulation.

The police found no sign of a forced entry, and were unable to find the acid container. The following morning, however, a bloodstained axe was discovered in the side yard of the adjoining property; it appeared to have been thrown from one of Place's windows.

Inquiries revealed that Martha was William Place's second wife; his first had died when Ida was eleven, and he had married Martha a year later, after employing her as a housekeeper for some months. There had been many bitter quarrels between them, Martha behaving so aggressively that her husband, a year earlier, had brought charges against her, though without success.

The police also learnt from Hilda Jans, who had been a servant in the house, that she had been dismissed from her position on the day of the murder, being given a month's wages in lieu of notice, together with a bonus of $5 for having packed in readiness to leave by 5 p.m.

Asked about the smell of carbolic acid, Hilda said that she had been out in the back yard after breakfast and had first noticed it when she returned to the house around 9.15 a.m. She had not seen Ida Place afterwards, and had later found her bedroom door locked.

As soon as he regained consciousness William Place, not realizing that Ida was dead or that his wife was a patient in the same hospital, told police that Martha had tried to kill him and begged them to protect his daughter.

When he was well enough to speak to them at greater length he said that Martha had complained of Ida showing her neither affection nor respect, and resented the way in which he indulged her; that was one of their differences. Another was Martha's practice of hoarding money in her own bank account and, at the same time, running up excessive bills for him to pay.

On the day that she attacked him, he said, he had arrived home from his office to find the house in darkness.

He let himself in, calling out to his wife, his daughter and the servant — for he did not know that Hilda had been dismissed, and then, hearing nothing, went to look in the kitchen. He was going back towards the front door when he heard somebody creeping down the stairs, and, turning round, saw that it was Martha. He spoke to her, unaware that she had an axe in her hand, but she suddenly rushed forward and began to strike him with it.

The police, after listening to his account, had the unpleasant duty of informing him that his daughter had been murdered.

They were now satisfied that Martha had planned to kill both her husband and her stepdaughter, and that she had tried to kill herself when she realized that William's cries for help had been loud enough to be heard by the neighbours. She was therefore charged and taken into custody.

On 5 July she was brought to trial, dressed entirely in black. She admitted the attacks, pleading intense provocation in each case, but refused to say where she had obtained the acid or how long it had been in her possession. She was found guilty, with no recommendation of mercy, and on 20 March 1899, she was executed in Sing Sing Prison.

She was the first woman ever to die in the electric chair.

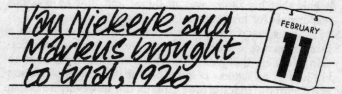

Van Niekerk and Markus brought to trial, 1926

FEBRUARY
11

On 11 February 1926, two ex-convicts, Andries Van Niekerk and Edward Markus, were brought to trial in Pretoria, accused of murdering the two occupants of a Transvaal farmhouse on the night of 2 December previously. The crime had been a callous one, and the farmhouse had been set on fire afterwards. The trial, which lasted eight days, was therefore followed with much interest.

Waterval Farm, in the Transvaal's Potgietersrust district, had been managed by sixty-year-old Bill Nelson for its absent owner; Nelson's companion, Tom Denton, a fifty-five-year-old former soldier, had run a small general store on the property, selling goods to its native workers. Both were evidently kind and friendly men, for when the two ex-convicts appeared at the farm in search of work they were treated with sympathy and generosity.

Nelson hired them to decorate the outside walls of the farm and gave them food and beds. He did not expect them to start work on the day of their arrival, and the next day he and Denton took them on a shooting trip, providing them with guns. On the evening of the second day they all dined together and retired early. Then, just after midnight, the sound of shots was heard, but nobody went to the scene until it was realized that the buildings were on fire. Two men were then seen running away from the premises.

Van Niekerk, aged thirty-four, was a habitual criminal with a long history of housebreaking, theft and violence: he had spent nearly half his life in prison and had been whipped on a number of occasions. A man of low mentality, he had delusions of persecution and superiority, and was given to outbursts of fury. It was contended on his behalf that his sanity was in doubt and that he was not responsible for his actions.

Markus, aged twenty-four, was a weaker man with a shorter record. On being arrested, he had made a confession, claiming that Van Niekerk — who had threatened to kill him — was solely responsible for the deaths of Nelson and Denton. Under cross-examination, however, he began to contradict himself, and it soon appeared that a confession which Van Niekerk had made in revenge — 'both Markus and I committed the crime' — was more credible.

Towards the close the question of whether Van Niekerk

was in such a condition that he would not know the nature and quality of his actions was put to a medical expert. The witness replied, 'I have seen an imbecile of the mental age of three or four years commit an act and know it was wrong. Therefore a person of higher age must know it.'

After an absence of just over two hours the jury found both defendants guilty and they were sentenced to death. Van Niekerk, pleased that Markus was to suffer the same fate as him, then waved his handkerchief towards relatives in the courtroom. The prisoners were both hanged on 14 April 1926.

Henry Smith found murdered, 1896

FEBRUARY
14

On the morning of 14 February 1896, Henry Smith, a seventy-nine-year-old widower, was found dead in the kitchen of his neglected mansion in Muswell Hill, north London. He had been struck on the head twelve times during the course of a struggle and had afterwards been bound and gagged, his attackers evidently not realizing that they had killed him. His bedroom had been ransacked and money had been taken from his safe.

The culprits had entered the house through a kitchen window after trying unsuccessfully to open two other windows with a jemmy, and Mr Smith, awakened by the noise, had come downstairs in his nightshirt to investigate. Two penknives, which had been used to cut strips from a tablecloth, were found beside the body; the intruders had also left behind a toy lantern. Mr Smith's body had been found by his gardener.

Police investigating the crime soon learnt that two

strange men had been seen in the neighbourhood during the previous two days, and these were seen as the most likely suspects. Further inquiries revealed that they were Henry Fowler, aged thirty-one, and Albert Milsom, thirty-three, two known criminals from Kentish Town who were both missing from their homes. The toy lantern found at the scene of the crime was identified by Milsom's fifteen-year-old brother-in-law as his own. A warrant was then obtained for the arrest of both men, and they were apprehended in Bath on 12 April.

Fowler, an ex-convict who had been released on licence on 16 January previously, was a tough individual; he resisted arrest and was not overpowered until he had been struck several times over the head with a police revolver. But his companion, a shifty little man, gave no trouble and afterwards made a statement in which he admitted the robbery and accused Fowler of the murder. Fowler, he said, had killed the old man while he (Milsom) was outside the house. He also revealed that he and Fowler had buried their burglary tools in the grounds of the mansion.

Infuriated by what he saw as an act of betrayal, Fowler claimed that the murder had been committed by Milsom; the 'dirty dog' had put his foot on the old man's neck and made sure that he was dead, he declared. Besides the evidence of the toy lantern and their own statements, they were both identified as the men who had been seen in the neighbourhood two days before the discovery of the crime, and a £10 note found in Fowler's possession was known to have been stolen from the victim's home.

Their trial began at the Old Bailey on 19 May and lasted three days, the judge remarking in his summing up that the evidence of the two penknives indicated that two people had been engaged in tying up Mr Smith. When the jury retired to consider their verdict, Fowler fell upon Milsom and tried to strangle him. He had to be forcibly restrained by warders and policemen, the struggle continuing for twelve minutes. The jury returned a verdict of guilty against each of them and they were sentenced to death.

Henry Fowler and Albert Milsom were hanged at Newgate Prison on 9 June 1896, together with another murderer named Seaman, who was placed between them on the scaffold. An accident occurred at the execution, the hangman's assistant falling through the trap with the condemned. But he escaped unhurt, having instinctively grasped the legs of the prisoner in front of him.

It was the last triple execution to be carried out at Newgate.

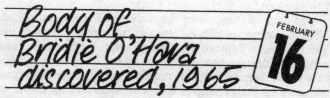

Body of Bridie O'Hara discovered, 1965

FEBRUARY 16

On 16 February 1965, the body of a naked woman was found in a patch of bracken on the Heron Trading Estate in Acton, west London. Bridie O'Hara, a twenty-seven-year-old prostitute of Agate Road, Hammersmith, had died of suffocation after an unsuccessful attempt at strangling; some of her teeth were missing and sperm was found in her throat. It appeared that she had died in a kneeling position, and also that her body had been kept somewhere cool before being taken to the place where it was found. Bridie O'Hara, a native of Dublin, had last been seen alive five weeks earlier.

At the time of this discovery police were investigating the cases of seven other prostitutes who had died mysteriously in the London area during the previous six years. The first of these, Elizabeth Figg, aged twenty-one, had been found strangled beside the Thames between Barnes and Chiswick on 17 June 1959; the skeleton of the second, Gwynneth Rees, aged twenty-two, during the clearing of a rubbish dump at Mortlake, also beside the Thames, on 8

November 1963. In the case of Gwynneth Rees the cause of death had not been established with certainty, but the fact that she too, had been a prostitute caused police to wonder whether the two cases were connected.

The other five bodies had all be found in 1964: Hannah Tailford, thirty, in the Thames at Hammersmith on 2 February; Irene Lockwood, twenty-six, also in the Thames (about 300 yards from the same place) on 9 April; Helene Barthelemy, twenty-two, near a sports ground in Brentford on 24 April; Mary Fleming, thirty, outside a garage near Chiswick High Road on 14 July, and Margaret McGowan, twenty-one, behind a car park in Kensington on 25 November.

In each of these cases the body had been found naked. There was no specific evidence of murder in two of them, for Hannah Tailford may have committed suicide, and Irene Lockwood had died from drowning. But the police regarded them as probable murder cases just the same, and when a caretaker named Kenneth Archibald confessed to having killed Irene Lockwood, he was arrested and brought to trial. He was found not guilty, having retracted his confession in the meantime.

In the case of Mary Fleming the body had been found in a sitting position in a cul-de-sac, close to a site where painters had been working the previous night. The painters had seen a man standing near a van, and when he became aware of their presence he had driven away hurriedly, almost colliding with a car. Though the driver of the car had reported the matter to the police, he had failed to make a note of the van's registration number, so the suspect could not be traced.

The deaths of Helene Barthelemy, Mary Fleming, and Margaret McGowan were all similar to that of Bridie O'Hara: teeth were missing from the bodies — false teeth in the case of Mary Fleming — and sperm was found in each of their throats. Traces of paint of a type used for spraying cars were found on the body in each case, leading police to speculate that they had been left in a garage or factory at some stage.

It seemed that the killer was a pervert who enjoyed strangling or choking his victims during oral sex, then repeating the sexual act later after forcing out some of their teeth. The fact that he removed all articles of clothing from the dead bodies led to him being called 'Jack the Stripper'.

The police were already engaged in a large-scale operation aimed at catching him, but it was not until the death of Bridie O'Hara that they located the place where the bodies had been kept — a transformer building near a paint-spray shop on the estate where Bridie O'Hara had been discovered.

The police then concentrated their efforts on the estate itself, taking note of all the vans seen in the area and paying particular attention to any which appeared there more than once. It was hinted on television that they were very near to bringing the culprit to justice. But, in fact, they never did so.

It was later claimed that one of the three main suspects, a forty-five-year-old security guard whose rounds included the paint-spray shop, had committed suicide while inquiries at the Heron Trading Estate were in progress. The man, who was unmarried, was not named, and his identity has not been made known to the public since. It is known, however, that he left a note saying he was 'unable to stand the strain any longer'.

With his death this shocking series of murders came to an end.

Murder of Mrs Durand-Deacon, 1949

On 18 February 1949, John George Haigh, aged thirty-nine, a resident at the Onslow Court Hotel in South Kensington, London, committed the crime for which he was to be hanged. It was by no means his first offence, for Haigh was a professional criminal who lived by fraud and theft and had resorted to murder several times before. To the other residents at the hotel, however, he was a man of charm and good manners who appeared to have made a success of running his own engineering business. They had no reason to suspect him of any wrong-doing.

His victim, Mrs Olive Durand-Deacon, was a rich widow of sixty-nine. She and Haigh were on friendly terms as a result of having adjacent tables in the dining-room, and when she told him of a scheme to manufacture artificial finger-nails of her own design he suggested that she visit his factory in Crawley, Sussex, where she could chose the necessary materials. This idea appealed to Mrs Durand-Deacon, and she agreed to go with him.

On the day in question they left London about 2.30 p.m., travelling in Haigh's Alvis car. About 4.15 p.m. they were seen together at the George Hotel in Crawley. But that was the last time that Mrs Durand-Deacon was seen by anyone except Haigh.

Haigh's 'factory', in Leopold Road, was actually a building which he did not own, but was occasionally allowed to use as a storeroom in connection with his 'experimental engineering' work. It contained various articles, including three carboys of sulphuric acid, a forty-five gallon drum which had been specially lined to hold corrosive chemicals, a stirrup pump, a pair of gloves and a rubber apron. If Mrs Durand-Deacon found any of these things suspicious, it did not prevent her turning her back on him, for Haigh, taking a revolver from his pocket, was able to kill her with a single shot in the back of the neck. He then removed all her valuables — a Persian lamb coat, rings, a necklace, earrings and a cruciform — before putting the body into the drum. The sulphuric acid was put in afterwards with the use of the stirrup pump.

Haigh immediately set about disposing of the valuables and paying off debts, returning to Crawley several times in the next few days in order to make sure that the body was dissolving in the acid. In the meantime he was obliged to go to the police, in the company of another resident, to report his victim's disappearance.

The police were suspicious of Haigh from the start, and were not surprised to learn that he had served three terms of imprisonment. Searching the 'factory' in Crawley, they found his revolver, some ammunition and a receipt for a Persian lamb coat which had been left at a cleaners' in Reigate. They also traced the victim's jewellery, which had been sold to a jeweller in Horsham, a few miles away.

On being taken to Chelsea police station for questioning, Haigh told the police how he had dissolved Mrs Durand-Deacon's body, evidently in the mistaken belief that if the body could not be found a murder charge could not be brought against him. An examination of the sludge outside the storeroom then led to the discovery of a human gallstone and some fragments of bone, showing that the disintegration had not been complete. These remains were later identified as those of Mrs Durand-Deacon.

Charged with the murder, Haigh confessed that he had also killed a Mr William Donald McSwann in London in 1944, Mr McSwann's parents, also in London, in 1945, and a Dr Archibald Henderson and his wife in Crawley in 1948. He claimed that he had committed these murders, like that of Mrs Durand-Deacon, because he wanted to drink the blood of the victims, but it was found that his real motive in each case had been financial gain.

He later claimed to have killed three other people, all of

whom were strangers to him, but the existence of these people was never proved.

At his trial in Lewes, in July 1949, for the murder of Mrs Durand-Deacon, Haigh pleaded that he was insane. The jury, however, took only fifteen minutes to reject this defence and returned a verdict of guilty. Haigh's execution took place at Wandsworth Prison on 6 August.

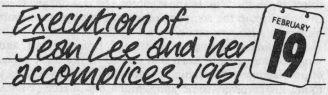

Execution of Jean Lee and her accomplices, 1951

On 19 February 1951, Jean Lee, a thirty-three-year-old Australian murderess, and her two accomplices, Robert David Clayton and Norman Andrews, were hanged for the murder of William Kent, a bookmaker aged seventy-three, in his hotel room in Carlton, New South Wales, in November 1949.

Jean Lee, an attractive woman, had taken to prostitution during the Second World War after the failure of her marriage; Clayton, her lover, was a petty criminal who lived off her earnings from the servicemen of various nations who were stationed in Australia at the time.

After the war they turned to blackmail, Jean Lee enticing men into compromising situations, and Clayton, pretending to be her irate husband, bursting in on them to demand compensation. Andrews, a thug, did not join them in their criminal activities until 1949.

The murder of William Kent took place on the night of 7 November. Jean Lee and her companions met him in the bar of his hotel and later she retired to his room with him and got him drunk so that she could pick his pockets. However, the old man kept a tight grip on his money and she was unable to get it away from him until she hit him on the head with a bottle. She then tied him up and let Clayton and Andrews into the room.

The two ruffians tied the old man's thumbs together with a bootlace, kicked him repeatedly and slashed him several times with a broken bottle before he finally died. The room was ransacked.

After the discovery of the body, members of the hotel staff gave descriptions of the three culprits to the police and they were soon identified and arrested in Sydney. They all made confessions and were brought to trial in March 1950, a retrial being granted as a result of the manner in which two of the confessions had been obtained. The second trial had the same result as the first, and the High Court confirmed the death sentences passed on each of them.

Their executions took place at Pentridge Jail.

Attempted execution of John Lee, 1885

FEBRUARY 23

On 23 February 1885, John Lee, a prisoner in Exeter Jail, was due to be hanged for the murder of Emma Keyse, an elderly spinster of Babbacombe, near Torquay, by whom he had been employed as a footman. The body of his victim had been discovered during the course of a fire at her home in the early hours of 15 November previously. Her throat had been cut so deeply that the vertebrae of her neck were notched; she had also been beaten over the head with a hatchet. Lee, a young man with a prison record for theft, had killed her because she had found fault with his conduct and reduced his wages from 2s 6d (12½p) to 2s (10p) a week. He had afterwards set fire to the house, probably in the hope of concealing the crime.

As the time appointed for his execution approached, Lee showed no sign of fear; the strain which the imminence of such an event always produced among the prison staff did not affect him at all. Just before 8 a.m. he was taken from his cell and the solemn procession to the scaffold began, the chief warder leading the way. Lee, accompanied by two other warders, walked behind the prison chaplain, the Reverend John Pitkin. Various officials, including the hangman, the prison governor and the under-sheriff, together with several more warders followed.

At the place of execution Lee's legs were strapped together and the white cap pulled over his face. James Berry, the hangman, then adjusted the rope round his neck and asked if he had anything to say. Lee replied that he had not. As the chaplain concluded his service the hangman pulled the lever which operated the two trap-doors. To everyone's amazement, they failed to open. The prisoner remained motionless.

Berry moved the lever to and fro, but the trap-doors still would not open. John Lee was removed from the scaffold to an adjoining room while an examination of the drop was carried out, and certain adjustments were made. Then the condemned was brought back and placed on the scaffold again. But when the hangman pulled the lever, the result was the same as it had been before: the trap-doors would not budge.

Once again the culprit was taken from the scaffold, this time to the prison basement. Further adjustments were made. After a few more minutes the prisoner was brought back for a third attempt, the drop having been tested and found to be in working order. The chaplain started the service for the third time. James Berry pulled the lever. But the trap-doors still remained closed. The third attempt had failed, too.

Everyone concerned, except the condemned, was now in a state of consternation. They had no idea what to do for the best. Finally, the chaplain told the under-sheriff that he would have nothing more to do with the execution. It had therefore to be postponed, as it could not be carried out without the chaplain being present. Mr Pitkin accompanied the prisoner as he was taken back to his cell.

Outside the prison, there was much surprise when the black flag did not appear, and this was followed by great excitement when it was heard that there had been three unsuccessful attempts to hang the prisoner. Newspaper offices were afterwards besieged by people wanting to know the latest news of the affair, and it was said that there was a general feeling that the prisoner's life should be spared after the ordeal which he had suffered. It was announced later the same day that John Lee had been reprieved and that his sentence would be commuted to life imprisonment.

The failure of the scaffold has never been satisfactorily explained. Some said it was caused by damp, others that it was due to faulty construction.

John Lee remained in prison for the next twenty-two years, and was released on 18 December 1907. The following year he published a book about his life, making himself out to be innocent of the murder of which he had been convicted. It sold well, but was not taken seriously by people acquainted with the case. His guilt had been too firmly established by the evidence.

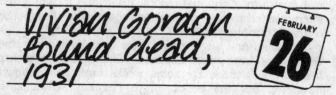

Vivian Gordon found dead, 1931

FEBRUARY 26

On the morning of 26 February 1931, Vivian Gordon, an attractive divorcée with expensive tastes, was found dead in a ravine in New York City's Van Cortlandt Park, having been strangled with a piece of clothes-line some hours earlier. Her mink coat, diamond ring and $665 wrist-watch were all missing, giving the impression that robbery had been the motive for the murder. However, the discovery of a five-volume diary in her Manhattan apartment, together with other pieces of evidence obtained elsewhere, caused police to suspect that this was not the case at all.

Vivian Gordon, who had once been convicted on a vice charge and sent to a reformatory, was found to have been both a blackmailer and a money-lender. It was also found that a few days before her murder she had given information to a committee investigating police corruption in New York City, claiming that her conviction eight years earlier had been the result of fabricated evidence. It therefore appeared that any one of a good many people could have had cause to want her out of the way.

The crime proved to be New York's most sensational murder for five years, with several well-known figures being regarded as suspects and many lurid details of the victim's life published. At one point the lawyer Bernard Gervase and a thief known as 'Knucklehead' Kaufman were arrested on suspicion, only to be released later. All this became too much for Vivian's sixteen-year-old daughter in New Jersey, and drove her to suicide.

Eventually it was discovered that in July 1929 Vivian Gordon had made a loan of $1500 to an ex-convict named Howie Schramm — known to her as Charles Reuben — and that this had never been repaid. Schramm, aged thirty-two, had a long criminal record, his crimes including the attempted strangling of a Bronx housewife during the course of a robbery in 1921.

Schramm and an associate — a thief named Dutchie Ginsman — were placed under surveillance, but no further headway was made for some weeks until an unknown informant put the police on to Herman Schwartz, a garment jobber, who said that Schramm had tried to sell him a mink coat, and had also had a diamond ring and an expensive wrist-watch for sale, on the morning of 26 February. Turning down the offer because the pelts were marked on the inside, Schwartz had taken Schramm to meet a diamond dealer and a Broadway dressmaker. The police officers investigating the crime had no doubt that the valuables in question had been those stolen from Vivian Gordon.

Another associate of Schramm's was found to be Harvey Sawyer, a young man with no criminal record. It was learnt that he had hired a Cadillac on the night of 25 February and returned it the following morning, and also that Schramm had been giving him occasional sums of money. When Schramm and Ginsman were finally interrogated in connection with the murder, they denied all knowledge of it. But Sawyer made a confession.

He revealed that the murder of Vivian Gordon had been planned beforehand, and that Schramm had taken her to Van Cortlandt Park — where Ginsman and Sawyer were waiting in the hired car — believing that she was to meet a potential victim of her own. Having introduced her to Ginsman, Schramm had got into the back of the car with her and strangled her there as they drove towards the ravine where her body was found.

Sawyer, whose own part in the affair had been confined to hiring and driving the car, believed that the murder had been carried out on behalf of 'Knucklehead' Kaufman. He also revealed that Schramm had been unable to sell the mink coat and had therefore burnt it.

Schramm and Ginsman were charged with murder and brought to trial in June 1931. Sawyer, Schwartz, the diamond dealer and the dressmaker all gave evidence, and it appeared that the prosecution's case was overwhelming. But then Howie Schramm's twenty-two-year-old sister appeared for the defence, stating that her brother had taken her out on the night of the murder and had remained in her company until daylight the following morning.

Ginsman's sister then gave *him* an alibi, testifying that he had spent the night at her home in the East Bronx. In this, she was supported by her sixteen-year-old son and a neighbouring shopkeeper.

To the amazement and disgust of the district attorney and the police officers concerned, the jury found both defendants not guilty. The case therefore remains officially unsolved.

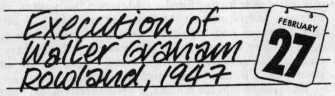

Execution of Walter Graham Rowland, 1947

FEBRUARY 27

On 27 February 1947, Walter Graham Rowland, a thirty-nine-year-old labourer, was hanged at Strangeways Prison for the murder of Olive Balchin, a prostitute aged about forty, whose body had been found on a bomb-site in Cumberland Street, near Deansgate, Manchester, on 20 October previously. The crime had been committed with a cobbler's hammer, which the culprit had left a few feet from the body, and had evidently taken place because Rowland was suffering from venereal disease and believed he had contracted it from the victim.

Rowland had been in trouble before and had, in fact, occupied the condemned cell at Strangeways on an earlier occasion. At the age of nineteen he had been sent to Borstal for three years for attempting to strangle sixteen-year-old Annie Schofield whom he married after being released; then, in 1934, he had strangled their daughter Mavis, aged two, with a stocking, and been sentenced to death. This latter sentence had been commuted to life imprisonment, and Rowland remained in jail until 1940, when he was freed after volunteering to serve in the army.

Demobilized from the Royal Artillery in June 1946, Rowland went to stay at the Services Transit Dormitory in

Manchester, and it was there that police went to find him after learning that he had been behaving suspiciously. 'You don't want me for murdering that woman, do you?' he asked, on being woken up. He admitted knowing Olive Balchin and said he suspected that she had given him venereal disease, but denied having killed her.

However, he was identified by a dealer in second-hand goods from whom he had bought the hammer, and also by two people who had seen him in the company of Olive Balchin on the night of 19 October. Two hairs found on Rowland's jacket matched the victim's own hair; a blood-stain on one of his shoes proved to be of the same group as Olive Balchin's blood. Moreover, samples of brick-dust, cement, charcoal and clinker from the turn-ups of his trousers matched other samples taken from the site where the body had been found.

While Rowland was awaiting trial on this occasion his wife divorced him on the grounds of cruelty. The divorce court had to sit *in camera* so that the jury at the forthcoming murder trial would not be prejudiced by disclosure of the prisoner's criminal record.

Rowland appeared for trial at the Manchester Assizes in December 1946, the case lasting five days. When the jury returned a verdict of guilty, he made a speech from the dock, claiming that he was innocent. 'The killing of this woman was a terrible crime, but there is a worse crime being committed now because someone with the knowledge of this murder is seeing me sentenced today for a crime which I did not commit,' he declared.

The case was made all the more extraordinary on 22 January 1947, when somebody else confessed to the murder of Olive Balchin. David John Ware, a thirty-nine-year-old man with a history of mental illness, was serving a sentence for theft at the time of Rowland's trial and sent his confession to the prison governor. He later retracted it, admitting that he had lied for the sake of publicity. In the meantime an inquiry had been held to discover whether there were grounds for thinking that Rowland's conviction

65

had been a miscarriage of justice. It concluded that there were no such grounds. Rowland nonetheless persisted in denying his guilt to the end.

Four years later David John Ware was tried for the attempted murder of another woman and found guilty but insane. He was sent to Broadmoor, where he committed suicide in April 1954.

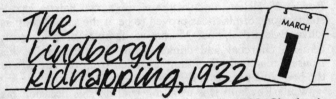

The Lindbergh kidnapping, 1932

Between 8 p.m. and 10 p.m. on 1 March 1932, Charles A. Lindbergh Jr, twenty-month-old son of the famous aviator, was abducted from his nursery at the Lindbergh Estate in the Sourland Mountains of Hunterdon County, New Jersey. The nursery was on the second floor of the house, and the child's disappearance was discovered by his Scots nurse, Betty Gow; a ransom note, demanding $50,000, was found on the window-sill.

The kidnapper had used a crudely-made ladder to gain access to the nursery, and had left no fingerprints. The ransom note — which was followed by another on 6 March increasing the demand to $70,000 — contained spelling mistakes, and was believed to have been written by a German of little education.

Colonel Lindbergh appealed to the kidnapper to start negotiations, and appointed Dr John F. Condon of the Bronx, New York, to act as an intermediary. The kidnapper sent Condon a note saying that he was agreeable to this, and later, at a meeting, gave his name as John. He sent Condon the missing child's night clothes as proof that he was the person concerned.

At a second meeting, in a cemetery in the Bronx in April, Condon offered 'John' $50,000 for the child's return. The offer was accepted and the money handed over, 'John' giving Condon a note informing him that the child was to be found on a boat called *Nellie* anchored off Martha's Vineyard, Massachusetts. He then hurried away in the darkness.

Colonel Lindbergh set off immediately, and the following day a search was carried out in the area indicated. But there was no sign of either the child or the boat. On 12 May the child's body was found in a shallow grave about five miles from the Lindbergh Estate. He had been killed by a blow on the head about two months earlier.

On 18 September 1934, a cashier at a petrol station in the Bronx received a note from a customer which he recognized as part of the ransom money. He informed the police, and the following day Bruno Richard Hauptmann, a former machine-gunner in the German army who had entered the United States illegally in 1923, was arrested. More of the ransom money was found in his possession, and his handwriting was found to be the same as that on the ransom notes. It was also discovered that he had a criminal record in Germany, his known offences including robbery and burglary.

Hauptmann was brought to trial for murder and kidnapping in January 1935. The proceedings lasted six weeks, and on 13 February he was found guilty on both charges. He was executed in the electric chair at Trenton State Prison, New Jersey, at the age of thirty-six, on 3 April 1936.

In January 1983 it was reported that his widow, Anna Hauptmann, aged eighty-four, was seeking damages for his death, and had accused the State of New Jersey and several former state and federal officials of conspiring to wrongfully convict an innocent man.

Klaus Grabowski brought to trial, 1981

On 3 March 1981, Klaus Grabowski, a thirty-five-year-old butcher with a history of child-molesting, was brought to trial in Lübeck, West Germany, charged with the murder of seven-year-old Anna Bachmeier. The child had failed to return home after going out to play in the morning of 5 May the previous year, and Grabowski, who lived only a block away, was later held for questioning in connection with her disappearance. He eventually confessed to having killed Anna, and led police to a piece of waste ground where her body was found. She had been strangled with her own tights.

Grabowski denied that the crime had been a sex murder and his counsel demanded that the charge be reduced to one of manslaughter. It was stated in court that following an earlier offence — his second — he had agreed to be castrated, but later had his sex drive restored by means of hormone injections. Omitting to explain why he had taken off Anna's tights, he claimed that he had had no sexual feelings towards her. He had invited her to his apartment because he loved children, and had killed her in a panic because she tried to blackmail him, he said.

All this was too much for Marianne Bachmeier, the child's mother. After listening to the case for three days in an apparently calm collected manner, she suddenly crossed the courtroom on 6 March, pulled out a Beretta pistol and fired seven bullets into the prisoner, killing him instantly. Frau Bachmeier, a former barmaid, then lowered the gun and waited passively to be arrested. The scene was witnessed by schoolgirls on an educational visit to the court, who began to cry hysterically. Later the same day the public prosecutor announced that Marianne Bachmeier was to be charged with murder.

Frau Bachmeier's life had not been a happy one even before Anna's death. The daughter of a former SS officer, she had been sexually assaulted at the age of nine and thrown out of home when she became pregnant at sixteen. Two years later she was raped while pregnant for the second time, the father in this case being a different man. Of the two children, one had been adopted, the other placed in an orphanage.

When these facts were reported, public sympathy, which was already strongly in her favour, became overwhelming, and large sums of money were donated to the defence fund started on her behalf. However, this sympathy began to wane when it was learnt that her fellow prisoners found her arrogant and suspected that she did not really care about Anna at all. Even so, when her trial began in November 1982, it was followed with intense interest.

Marianne Bachmeier — 'the Avenging Mother', as the press called her — was convicted of manslaughter on 2 March 1983, and sentenced to six years' imprisonment. The trial judge, in an hour-long account of his findings, said that she had not planned to kill Grabowski but decided to do so when she saw him sitting in the dock. The defence had earlier claimed that she had bought the pistol with the intention of committing suicide.

She was released on parole in June 1985.

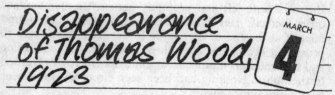

Disappearance of Thomas Wood, 1923

MARCH 4

On 4 March 1923, Thomas Wood, aged three, was reported missing from his home in Glossop, a coal-mining town in Derbyshire. The report led to a search of the town and surrounding countryside, but no trace of the missing child was found. The circulation of his description to other districts, in the hope that he might be found wandering further afield, brought no results; likewise, the dragging of the River Goyt, which runs through Glossop, revealed nothing. After the search had been going on for nine days, a local man went to the police and told them that he knew something about the boy's disappearance.

Albert Edward Burrows, a farm labourer, said that on the day in question, a Sunday, he had taken Thomas Wood for a walk to Simmondley, a village about a mile from Glossop. He had left him on his own for a few minutes near a disused mineshaft on Symmondley Moor and then been unable to find him, he continued. He gave no satisfactory reason for having failed to report this earlier.

Burrows was already known to the police in connection with other offences. Four years earlier he had been sent to prison for bigamy after going through a ceremony of marriage with a woman from Nantwich, Cheshire, by whom he had had an illegitimate child. After returning to his lawful wife on release, he had been sent to prison again, this time for failing to pay maintenance to the child's mother.

The woman, Hannah Calladine, had another child, besides the one which Burrows had fathered. In December 1919, fourteen months after her second confinement, she suddenly turned up in Glossop with both children and all her belongings, and moved into Burrows' home. At this, Burrows' wife left and promptly obtained a maintenance order herself. Her husband, being a poor man, found himself at the age of fifty-seven in danger of being sent to prison yet again. But after three weeks Hannah Calladine and her children disappeared, and Mrs Burrows returned to the house. Nothing had been seen either of Hannah or her children since then.

With great difficulty, the police searched the mineshaft which Burrows had indicated, and eventually they recovered the body of Thomas Wood. He had been sexually assaulted and then murdered, probably by strangulation, before being thrown into the shaft.

The police, going to interview Burrows again, found him about to leave the house, perhaps for good. He stuck to the story he had told them before, but could not convince them he was telling the truth. On 28 March he was charged with murder.

While he was awaiting trial the police began to investigate the disappearance of Hannah Calladine and her children. It was learnt that on 11 January 1920, Burrows had taken Hannah and the younger child for a walk, and that this was the last time anyone else had seen them. Early the following morning he had taken the older child, a girl of four, for a walk — and that had been the last time anyone had seen her.

Six weeks after Burrows had been arrested the police began searching the mineshaft on Symmondley Moor again, and a fortnight later the remains of Hannah and her children were discovered there. They, too, had been murdered, probably by strangulation, though this could not be established with certainty. Burrows, who for three years had kept up a pretence that they were all still alive, was then charged with their murders.

He was brought to trial for the murder of Hannah and the younger child at the Derby Assizes in July 1923. The case against him included the evidence of another prisoner, whom Burrows had tried to persuade to forge a letter from Hannah, saying that she was still alive. The defence called no witnesses, but contended that Hannah had committed suicide. But Burrows was convicted and sentenced to death.

He was hanged in Nottingham, at the age of sixty-two, on 8 August 1923.

71

Murder of Gertrude Yates, 1922

On the morning of 6 March 1922, Gertrude Yates, a prostitute aged twenty-five, was found dead in the bathroom of her basement flat in Fulham, London. She had died of asphyxia, a towel having been rammed down her throat and a dressing-gown cord tied around her neck; she had also been beaten over the head with a blunt instrument. The body was naked.

In her bedroom, there was blood everywhere; a rolling-pin, with which the blows to her head had been inflicted, lay under the eiderdown. The dressing-table had been ransacked and some jewellery stolen. The body had been discovered by the victim's daily help, Miss Emily Steel, who knew Mrs Yates as Olive Young.

Miss Steel had arrived at the flat about 9.15 a.m., letting herself in with her own key. She had gone to the kitchen and started to cook sausages for her own breakfast, tidying the sitting-room as she did so. While she was thus occupied a man known to her as Major True entered the room and told her that Miss Young was still asleep and should not be disturbed, as they had had a late night together; he would send round his car for her at midday. He then put on his coat, with Miss Steel's help, and gave her half-a-crown (12¹/₂p) before leaving to get a taxi. Miss Steel found the body shortly afterwards and ran out to get help.

The man Miss Steel had seen in the flat was, in fact, Ronald True, a mentally-ill man of thirty who was not a major at all. He was already known to the police, his wife — who was alarmed at his deteriorating state of mind — having reported him missing only three days earlier. He was arrested at the Palace of Varieties in Hammersmith

72

within twelve hours of the body being discovered; the police found a loaded revolver in his hip pocket.

True, a former pupil at Bedford Grammar School, was a compulsive liar and a morphia addict. His stepfather, a wealthy man, had several times sent him abroad to learn work of some sort, but he was incapable of holding any job for long. In 1915 he joined the Royal Flying Corps, but on his solo flight he crashed the plane, suffering severe concussion. A month later he was involved in another crash. After his second spell in hospital he had a nervous breakdown, and was discharged from the service. He then worked briefly at one thing after another, in various countries, but finally his stepfather reconciled himself to giving him a regular allowance for doing nothing.

He was always popular with young women, and invariably managed to impress them with lies about himself. One such woman was an actress named Frances Roberts, whom he married soon after leaving the Royal Flying Corps. She, however, could not have been taken in for very long, for he was becoming increasingly abnormal and was regularly seeking treatment for his drug-addiction — treatment which never worked. In September 1921, he was fined in Portsmouth for using forged prescriptions to obtain morphia.

He began to talk about another Ronald True, an imaginary figure whom he believed to be his enemy. This 'other' Ronald True, he said, had been impersonating him and forging his signature on cheques which bounced. At the same time he was becoming violent towards his wife and hostile towards their two-year-old son. Suddenly, early in 1922, he decided to leave home.

For the next few weeks he stayed in hotels in London, frequenting clubs and bars in the West End and committing a variety of thefts. Though apparently having a good time, he was increasingly preoccupied with the 'other' Ronald True, and bought the gun that was later found in his possession in order to protect himself against this imaginary figure.

On the night of 5 March, just before midnight, he arrived at Gertrude Yates' flat in a chauffeur-driven car which he had been using for four days. He sent the driver away and stayed the night with Mrs Yates, from whom he had earlier stolen £5. In the morning he made tea for them both, then took Mrs Yates' cup into the bedroom; it was as she sat up to drink it that he attacked her with the rolling-pin. He afterwards drank his own cup of tea and ate some biscuits.

True was brought to trial at the Old Bailey in May 1922. He pleaded insanity, producing two psychiatrists to give evidence that he was suffering from a congenital mental disorder, aggravated by his addiction to morphia. But he was found guilty and sentenced to death.

Though his appeal was dismissed by the Lord Chief Justice, he was examined by three specialists on the orders of the Home Secretary and found to be insane. He was therefore reprieved and sent to Broadmoor.

He remained there for the rest of his life, a cheerful man who took part in the social activities and was popular with the other inmates. He died, at the age of sixty, in 1951.

Bodies of Dr. Petiot's victims found, 1944

MARCH
11

On 11 March 1944, a resident of the Rue Lesueur in Paris complained to the police about greasy black smoke coming from the chimney of a neighbouring house owned by Dr Marcel Petiot. The police arrived at the house to investigate and found a card pinned to the door, directing callers to an address in the Rue Caumartin where Dr Petiot lived and also had a consulting room. They contacted him by telephone.

Dr Petiot said that he would come to the Rue Lesueur immediately, but before he appeared the chimney caught fire and the fire brigade was called to the scene. Breaking into the house, the firemen entered the cellar, where a fire had been left to burn in a stove. There they found a large number of corpses, most of which had been dismembered.

When Petiot finally turned up he was told that he would be taken into custody. Unperturbed, he said that the bodies were those of pro-Nazis and collaborators killed by the French Resistance. The police were taken in by this, and made the mistake of letting Petiot go free. Petiot, his wife and their seventeen-year-old son promptly left their home in the Rue Caumartin and went into hiding. His wife was later found in Auxerre but Petiot managed to avoid being arrested for several months.

After the fall of Paris the newspapers gave a lot of publicity to the case, and Petiot wrote to one of them, stating that he was an officer of the Resistance and that the corpses found in his cellar had been placed there by the Gestapo. The handwriting of the letter was found to correspond with that of a Captain Henri Valéry, who had joined the Free French Forces just six weeks earlier and was serving in Reuilly. Petiot was thus discovered and arrested on 2 November.

On being taken to the Quai des Orfèvres for questioning, he said that as a member of the Resistance he had killed sixty-three people, and that the twenty-seven bodies in his cellar had been mostly those of German soldiers. He also said that he had helped many Frenchmen to escape from France. This time, however, nobody was taken in.

Marcel Petiot, a qualified doctor and former Mayor of Villeneuve, was a man with marked criminal tendencies. As a schoolboy he had stolen from his classmates; as an army conscript during the First World War he had stolen drugs from a casualty clearing station, and as Mayor of Villeneuve he had robbed his electric light meter and stolen from a municipal store. Later, in Paris, he was convicted of drug-trafficking and also of stealing a book.

The bodies discovered in his cellar were found to be the remains of people who had gone to his house with all their money and valuables, thinking that he would help them to escape from the Germans. They had each been given a lethal injection, then left in a sound-proofed room built specially for the purpose. Petiot had made himself a fortune out of all these murders; in all likelihood, he had also derived enjoyment from watching through a spyhole as his victims died in agony.

After seventeen months in custody, Petiot was brought to trial at the Seine Assize Court on twenty-seven charges of murder. The trial lasted three weeks and, on 4 April 1946, the jury returned verdicts of guilty on twenty-four of those charges. Petiot, aged forty-nine, was executed by guillotine on the morning of 26 May.

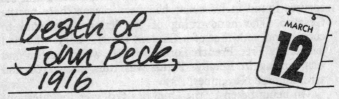

Death of John Peck, 1916

MARCH 12

On 12 March 1916, John Peck, a seventy-two-year-old timber millionaire of Grand Rapids, Michigan, died at the home of his son-in-law, Dr Arthur Warren Waite, a New York dentist. The cause of his death was diagnosed as a kidney disease and arrangements were made for the body to be cremated. But Peck's son Percy, whose mother had also died in Waite's home only a few weeks earlier, demanded its return to Michigan for burial, and afterwards requested an autopsy. When this was carried out, the body was found to contain arsenic.

Waite, aged twenty-seven, had studied at Glasgow University and worked in South Africa for some years before his marriage to Clara Peck in September 1915. In addition to having a dental practice in New York's fashionable Riverside Drive, he worked on germ-culture research at Cornell University. However, he lived extravagantly, having affairs with other women, and as his wife now inherited half of her father's fortune, he was suspected of having murdered both of her parents.

On 23 March the fashionable dentist was found suffering from an overdose of drugs, having apparently tried to take his own life. When he recovered he was charged with the murders of John and Hannah Peck and later brought to trial. Having pleaded not guilty, he then made an extraordinary confession, stating not only that he had murdered both of his wife's parents, but also that he had intended to murder his wife as well.

He had murdered his mother-in-law by putting diphtheria, tuberculosis and influenza germs in her food, he explained. He had then used the same methods in an attempt to kill his father-in-law, even using a nasal spray containing tuberculosis bacteria in his case. When these and other attempts proved unsuccessful, he had finally disposed of John Peck with the use of arsenic.

Waite revealed that it was for the sake of their money that he had murdered Clara's parents, and said that he would have murdered Clara next because he intended to have a more beautiful wife. Asked if he was crazy, he replied, 'I think not — unless it is crazy to want money'.

It was nonetheless on grounds of insanity that appeals were made on his behalf when he was convicted and sentenced to death. But these were unsuccessful and his execution in the electric chair was carried out at Sing Sing Prison on the night of 24 May 1917.

Four poisoned in Lund, 1949

On 13 March 1949, two medical students and two children in Lund, Sweden, were taken ill as a result of eating chocolate which had been poisoned with arsenic. The two students, Odvar Eiken and Anders Muren, and one of the children recovered after receiving hospital treatment, but the other child died. The investigation which followed involved the police of Norway and Denmark, as well as Sweden.

Eiken and Muren, both Norwegians in their late twenties, were room-mates lodging with a family named Svendson, and Eiken was engaged to Muren's sister Randi — a student at a teachers' training college in Kristiansand, Norway — though their engagement had not yet been formally announced. The chocolate, which had been sent to Eiken through the post, appeared to have been a gift from Randi.

Odvar Eiken had given a little of the chocolate to Muren and eaten some of it himself; the rest had been given to his landlady's eight-year-old daughter Marianne who, in turn, had given some to her friend Barbro Jakobson. It was Marianne Svendson who failed to recover from its effects.

Randi Muren denied sending the chocolate to Eiken, but agreed that handwriting on the gift card which had accompanied it was similar to her own. She revealed that since making her engagement known to friends she had received a number of anonymous letters suggesting that her fiancé was having affairs with girls in Sweden, and a further letter from a woman named Signe Lundgren claiming that she was expecting Eiken's child. At the same time Eiken, who said that he did not know anybody named Signe Lundgren, had been receiving anonymous letters of the same type about her.

The investigating officers, both Swedish and Norwegian became convinced that these letters and the poisoned chocolate were connected, and — observing that Randi Muren was an extremely attractive girl — suggested that they might have been the work of a jealous rival. Further questions elicited the information that a young Dane named Flemming Rosbörg, who had worked in Norway for a year, had recently threatened to commit suicide after failing to persuade her to marry him. As his present whereabouts were unknown, the Copenhagen police were asked to make inquiries about him.

He was soon arrested and handed over to the Swedish police for questioning, but then released after giving a satisfactory account of his movements. In the meantime, it had been learnt that shortly before the arrival of the poisoned chocolate, Odvar Eiken had received (also through the post) a small bottle of whisky inside a cigar-box. He had been ill after drinking some of it, but had not realized that the illness was connected with the whisky. When the rest of the whisky was handed to the police, together with the cigar-box, it was found to contain arsenic.

Several women named Signe Lundgren had been traced, but none of them knew Odvar Eiken or Randi Muren. Nor could any other woman be found in Sweden to substantiate the accusations which had been made against Eiken. But then another case of arsenic poisoning was reported, this time in Kristiansand.

Carstein Brekke, a friend of Randi Muren and her fiancé who was also a student at the teachers' training college, claimed that he, too, had received chocolate through the post and been ill after eating some of it. He produced a box containing several pieces which were found to have been poisoned, though with smaller amounts of arsenic than the chocolate sent to Eiken. Brekke could think of no reason why anyone should want to poison him, other than the fact that he was a friend of the other victims, he said.

The matter was further complicated by the discovery of a paid advertisement which had appeared in a Stavanger newspaper, announcing that Carstein Brekke and Randi Muren had become engaged — which both parties said they were unable to explain. However, when a police officer showed Randi the cigar-box in which the poisoned whisky had been sent to Eiken, she said that it was Brekke who owned it.

Brekke, though a close friend of Randi's, also turned out to be another of her rejected suitors. A letter which he had sent to his mother on 13 March contained information about Eiken's poisoned chocolate, though this was not known by Randi until the following day. Moreover, a notebook which he had discarded was found to have been used for imitations of Randi's handwriting. After being questioned intensively for some hours, he admitted having sent Eiken the poisoned chocolate. However, he refused to allow a police officer to take down his confession, saying that he wanted to write it himself in a more intellectual manner.

The written statement which he then made gave details of an unsuccessful attempt to get Randi Muren — the only woman in his life, he claimed — to break off her engagement, followed by an equally unsuccessful attempt to poison his rival.

Charged on a number of counts, Carstein Brekke was brought to trial in Kristiansand in October 1949, and convicted of manslaughter and attempted murder. He was then sentenced to twelve years' imprisonment and ten years' loss of rights as a citizen. The sentence of imprisonment was later increased to fifteen years when the case was taken to the Norwegian Supreme Court.

Shooting of Gaston Calmette, 1914

On the afternoon of 16 March 1914, Henriette Caillaux, the wife of the French Finance Minister, entered the offices of the daily newspaper *Le Figaro* and asked to see Gaston Calmette, the editor-in-chief. That very morning *Le Figaro* had published a facsimile of an indiscreet love letter which Madame Caillaux had received from her husband before their marriage, and Calmette assumed that she would try to come to an arrangement with him to prevent the publication of other such letters which she knew to be in his possession. He therefore agreed to see her.

A moment later the sound of shots was heard, and other members of staff rushed into Calmette's office to see what had happened. They found him lying on the floor, covered with blood. Madame Caillaux made no attempt to escape. 'I shot Calmette deliberately because he wanted to destroy my husband and me,' she confessed to the police. The following day Calmette died of his wounds. Henriette Caillaux, one of the best-known women in Paris, was charged with his murder; she was brought to trial four months later.

Joseph Caillaux, a former Prime Minister, was a very unpopular man. The rich had hated him for years because, during an earlier period as Finance Minister, he had introduced an income tax. More recently he had become widely despised as a result of his opposition to the impending war with Germany.

Gaston Calmette had been the most implacable of his opponents. He had repeatedly accused Caillaux of betraying his country and, on acquiring some of the Finance Minister's private letters written during the course of his previous marriage, had been determined to use them to

81

bring about his downfall.

At her trial Henriette Caillaux said that the attacks on her husband had caused both of them much unhappiness. Joseph Caillaux, on learning that the letters were in Calmette's hands, had bought a pistol, saying that he would kill Calmette if they were published. She had been unable to get him to part with it.

On the day of the shooting, she claimed, she had found the newspaper on the breakfast table, her husband having left without waking her. She went to his desk, where she knew that the pistol was normally kept in a locked drawer, but found the drawer open and the gun missing. After two unsuccessful attempts to see him at his ministry she decided to confront Calmette, and bought a gun herself for the purpose of threatening him. She claimed — in spite of her original confession — that she had not intended to kill him.

The trial took place during the week preceding the declaration of war between Austria–Hungary and Serbia, and its outcome depended less on the events of 16 March than on the motives of Joseph Caillaux and Gaston Calmette. There were some sensational developments in this respect, and soon the case became — for a few days, at least — the main preoccupation of the whole country.

One of Calmette's editors told the court that documents proving that Caillaux had betrayed France had been placed in the hands of the President of the Republic. This was to be refuted the following day by a statement, authorized by the Government, that the President had received no such papers. In the meantime, Caillaux was called as a witness and caused much indignation.

'Calmette has accused me of betraying my country to the Germans,' he said. 'Therefore, I am forced to tell the truth. I state here and now that *Le Figaro* has accepted German money!'

The publisher of the newspaper, called to deny the allegation, was forced to concede that *Le Figaro* had German shareholders. The admission was made with the utmost reluctance.

Later, just before the closing speeches, Caillaux re-appeared with a copy of Calmette's will, revealing that the victim of the shooting had avoided paying taxes on a very large inheritance. He also produced a contract which had been drawn up between Calmette and the Government of Austria–Hungary, by which Calmette pledged himself to write articles serving the interests of that government in return for money. The presiding judge read the contract aloud, remarking that there could be no doubt about its authenticity.

These revelations caused an uproar in the court, with spectators leaping to their feet, crying out that Calmette had been a traitor and that shooting had been too good for him. The jury considered the case for only a quarter of an hour before returning a unanimous verdict of not guilty. Caillaux and his wife did not leave the court in triumph, however, for the verdict was immediately overshadowed by the news that Austria–Hungary and Serbia were at war.

Caillaux returned to his political life after an enforced withdrawal. He was later to be imprisoned by Clemenceau for corresponding with the enemy.

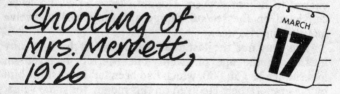

Shooting of Mrs. Merrett, 1926

MARCH 17

On the morning of 17 March 1926, Mrs Bertha Merrett, a woman of private means, was rushed to hospital from her furnished rooms in Buckingham Terrace, Edinburgh, with a bullet wound in her right ear; she was alive but unconscious. The wound appeared to have been self-inflicted, and when her son, John Donald Merrett, aged seventeen, informed the police that she had tried to kill herself because she was in financial difficulties, they saw no cause to disbelieve him.

Mrs Merrett was kept in isolation at the Royal Infirmary. When she recovered consciousness she was asked no questions about the bullet wound, but made a statement of her own accord to one of the doctors. 'I was sitting down, writing letters, and my son Donald was standing beside me,' she said. 'I said, "Go away, Donald, and don't annoy me." And the next thing I heard was a kind of explosion, and I don't remember anything more.' She died on 1 April.

Despite her statement, her death was regarded as suicide, until the discovery of one of her cheque-books in Donald Merrett's bedroom caused police officers to suspect otherwise. During the investigation which followed it was found that the signatures on many of Mrs Merrett's cheques had been forged. At the same time tests were carried out on the pistol that killed her.

Eventually, on 1 February 1927, Donald Merrett, now aged eighteen, was brought to trial in Edinburgh. He was charged with his mother's murder, and also with forging twenty-nine cheques on her account. The prosecution claimed that the absence of powder-blackening round the bullet wound proved that the gun had not been fired closely enough to be consistent with suicide, but the jury found the charge to be not proven. Donald Merrett was, however, convicted on the second charge and sentenced to twelve months' imprisonment.

This was not the last that was heard of him, by any means. At the age of twenty-one Merrett received an inheritance of £50,000, which had been left in trust for him by his grandfather. He lived on this money for some years, then, having spent most of it, returned to a life of crime. Now known as Ronald John Chesney, he committed a variety of offences — blackmail, fraud, theft and smuggling — before going into the Royal Naval Volunteer Reserve during the Second World War. After the war he lived in Germany, and was mainly engaged in black-market activities. Then, in 1954, he decided to murder his wife.

Merrett had married Vera Bonnar, the daughter of one of his mother's friends, in 1928. At the time of his inheritance he had made a settlement of £8400 on her, the money to revert to him in the event of her death. They had long since separated, and Vera Merrett, known as Vera Chesney, ran an old people's home in Ealing with her mother, who called herself Lady Menzies.

Merrett came to England in disguise, using a false passport. He visited his wife, got her hopelessly drunk, and drowned her in a few inches of water in her own bath, intending to make her death appear to have been the result of an accident. But as he was leaving the house he was seen by his mother-in-law, and realized that he would have to kill her too. After a desperate struggle he managed to overpower and strangle her. He then escaped from the house and flew back to Germany.

But he had been seen in the neighbourhood, and it was not long before the police were after him. On 16 February 1954, less than a week after the double murder, he was found dead in a wood near Cologne; he had shot himself. His arms were scratched and bruised from the struggle with his mother-in-law, and pink fibres from her scarf were found on his clothing. His German mistress, Gerda Schaller, said that Merrett had confided to her that he was guilty of the murder of his mother twenty-eight years earlier.

Murder of John Nisbet, 1910

MARCH
18

On the morning of 18 March 1910, John Nisbet, a forty-four-year-old cashier working for the Stobswood Colliery

Company, left his employers' Newcastle office to deliver £370 in wages to a colliery at Widdrington, thirty-five miles away. It was a journey he made every Friday, leaving Newcastle by train at 10.27 a.m. and carrying the money in a black leather bag. On this occasion, however, he did not alight at Widdrington because he was dead by the time the train arrived there. His body was discovered by a porter when the train reached Alnmouth.

Nisbet had been shot five times, his body hidden under a seat and the bag of money stolen. It was established that John Alexander Dickman, a former secretary of a colliery syndicate, had travelled in the same compartment, leaving the train at Morpeth. The post-mortem examination revealed that the bullets found in Nisbet's body had been fired from two different guns.

Dickman, a married man with two children, lived in Jesmond. He made his living out of betting on horses and was often in financial difficulties. It was also found that he had recently owned a revolver. He was therefore an obvious suspect.

On the day of the murder Dickman had had to pay excess fare at Morpeth, as he had only bought a ticket to Stannington, the previous stop. Asked to explain this, he told police that he had intended getting out at Stannington, in order to attend an interview for a job with the overseer at the Dovecot Moor colliery, but had gone on to Morpeth by mistake. This proved to be a lie, the overseer at Dovecot telling police that no such interview had been arranged.

Dickman was arrested and charged with murder. A search of his home failed to produce either of the guns, the black bag or any of the stolen money. But it was soon discovered that he had managed to pay off one or two debts to money-lenders almost immediately after the murder.

Brought to trial at the Newcastle Summer Assizes on 4 July, Dickman denied the offence. The case for the prosecution depended upon circumstantial evidence, but was strong enough to convince the jury of his guilt. He was sentenced to death.

On 9 July the black leather bag which had contained the stolen money was found in a disused mine-shaft between Morpeth and Stannington; it had been cut open — the key having been left in the victim's pocket — and all the money removed. Its discovery convinced the police that they had made no mistake in arresting Dickman. But the guns which had been used were never found.

There were many other people who felt that the evidence against Dickman was insufficient to warrant a conviction, and attempts were made to get him reprieved. But these were unsuccessful, and he was hanged at Newcastle Prison on 10 August 1910.

Albert Snyder found murdered, 1927
MARCH 20

Getting up on the morning of 20 March 1927, Lorraine Snyder, aged ten, of Queen's Village, Long Island, came out of her bedroom and found her mother lying bound and gagged at the top of the stairs. She let out a scream, then telephoned some neighbours, who immediately came to her assistance. On being untied, Ruth Snyder, aged thirty-two, said that she had been attacked and knocked unconscious by an intruder — a big man with a moustache, looking 'like an Italian' — who had entered her bedroom while she was asleep. She supposed that she must have been dragged out of the bedroom while she was still unconscious.

Entering the bedroom themselves, the neighbours found that Mrs Snyder's husband had been murdered. Albert Snyder, forty-four-year-old art editor of *Motor Boating* magazine, lay on the bed, his head having been so savagely battered that he was almost unrecognizable. When the police were called to the scene, it was also discovered that a piece of picture wire had been tied tightly round his neck and pieces of cotton wool, soaked in chloroform, stuffed into his mouth and nostrils. Clearly, it was a case of premeditated murder, and it was not long before the police began to have doubts about Ruth Snyder's story.

Searching the house for clues, they found pots and pans scattered about the kitchen and the contents of a bureau strewn about the living-room floor. But there was no sign of a forced entry. Jewels which Mrs Snyder claimed had been stolen were found hidden under her mattress, and some scraps of paper, pieced together, turned out to be a love letter which she had received from somebody signing himself 'Judd'. Ruth Snyder, on being questioned at length, then confessed that she had been having an affair with a salesman named Henry Judd Gray, who was an employee of the Bien Jolie Corset Company.

Gray, a timid man of thirty-five, was questioned about the murder, but denied having had anything to do with it. However, the police told Ruth Snyder that he had broken down and made a confession, blaming her for what had happened. She then made a statement, admitting that she had conspired with Gray to kill her husband but claiming that she had taken no part in the crime itself.

On being confronted with this, Gray made a statement, saying that they had committed the murder together, but that he had been under her influence at the time. 'She had this power over me,' he said. 'She told me what to do and I just did it.' Thus, the truth about what had happened gradually emerged.

Ruth Snyder and Judd Gray, both unhappily married, had begun to have an affair in 1925. Mrs Snyder disliked her husband, who often compared her unfavourably with a former fiancée, and had made a number of unsuccessful attempts to kill him on her own before finally getting Gray to help her. She had also taken out life insurance policies by which she stood to gain $96,000 after the murder had been carried out.

On the night of 19 March Gray entered the house while his mistress and her husband were out at a party. When they returned he kept himself concealed until after they had gone to bed. He then entered the bedroom and, taking Snyder by surprise, struck him over the head with a sash weight. After the murder Ruth Snyder helped to disarrange the room and allowed herself to be tied up and gagged before Gray left the house.

On 25 April the two prisoners were brought to trial for murder, the case being given a tremendous amount of publicity. As the sordid details were made known, Ruth Snyder was seen to be a callous schemer who had turned a weak man into a murderer by means of 'drink, veiled threats and intensive love'. As such, she became an object of fascination among ordinary people, and received 164 proposals of marriage.

The trial ended on 9 May with both defendants being found guilty; they were sentenced to death. Both were executed in the electric chair at Sing Sing Prison in January 1928.

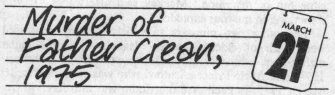

Murder of Father Crean, 1975

MARCH 21

On 21 March 1975, Father Anthony Crean, a Catholic priest, was brutally murdered at his home in Gravesend, Kent, his assailant striking him over the head with an axe and also stabbing him several times with a knife. The police suspected a twenty-two-year-old psychopath named Patrick Mackay, whose mother lived locally, and arrested him two days later. Mackay soon confessed, not only to that crime, but to two other murders as well, and was brought to trial for all three in November the same year. He was sentenced to life imprisonment.

Mackay, the son of a drunken clerk, had a long record of theft and violence. As a schoolboy, besides being a bully, a liar and a thief, he had taken to torturing animals and on one occasion had been put on probation for setting fire to a church. At thirteen he was admitted to a mental hospital after attacking his mother and sisters, and at fifteen — by which time he had committed a number of other violent crimes — he was described by a Home Office psychiatrist as 'a cold psychopathic killer'. Thereafter he became an admirer of the Nazis, drank heavily, took drugs and committed a great many burglaries and muggings.

In 1973 Father Crean, then aged sixty-three, befriended him, but not long afterwards Mackay broke into his house and stole a cheque. When he was arrested for this the priest tried to prevent him being prosecuted, and Mackay was merely fined £20 and set free.

On the day of the murder Mackay entered the house, which had been left open in Father Crean's absence. The victim, on returning, became nervous and tried to leave again, but Mackay attacked him and chased him into the bathroom, where further blows were struck. 'I must have gone out of my mind,' Mackay said afterwards. 'It was something in me that exploded.'

The other two murders to which Mackay confessed were both of elderly women: Isabella Griffiths, aged eighty-four, who was stabbed to death on 14 February 1974, and Adele Price, a widow, who was strangled on 10 March 1975. In each case the victim was murdered in her own home for no particular reason. 'I felt hellish and very peculiar inside,' said Mackay, referring to the murder of Adele Price.

Besides the three murders for which he was sent to prison, Mackay was believed to have committed eight others, but no charges were brought against him in connection with any of them.

Double murder in West Shelby, 1915

On the morning of 22 March 1915, Margaret Wolcott, a housekeeper, was found dead on her employer's farm at West Shelby, in Orleans County, New York; she had been shot with a revolver and was lying in her nightgown outside the door of a cottage occupied by Charles E. Stielow, a hired man. The farm-owner, Charles B. Phelps, aged seventy, lay in his nightshirt in the farmhouse kitchen, fatally injured, also by shooting; he died in hospital later, having been unable to speak from the time of his discovery. His desk had been broken open and all his money stolen.

Stielow, a thirty-seven-year-old German immigrant, lived with his wife, child, mother-in-law and brother-in-law; he was a strong but simple-minded man. Discovering what had happened, he had sent his brother-in-law, Nelson Green — who was equally simple minded — to inform the Orleans County Sheriff, Chester D. Bartlett. But he also got Green to hide his revolver, rifle and shotgun, as he was afraid that he might otherwise be accused of the murders himself.

The county had had no other serious crime within living memory, and the sheriff, having no idea how to conduct a murder investigation, hired an unscrupulous private detective named Newton, from Buffalo, to do it for him. Newton promptly had Green arrested, terrified him into revealing the whereabouts of his brother-in-law's guns, then forced him to make a confession that he and Stielow had killed Phelps and his housekeeper. Newton and Bartlett then arrested Stielow and had him interrogated for two days without food or sleep until he, too, confessed to the murders.

On 12 July Stielow was brought to trial. The stolen

money had not been recovered and the prisoner's confession, which he retracted, was regarded with suspicion by the judge. However, the prosecution introduced the evidence of a charlatan named Albert Hamilton, who purported to be a ballistics expert, as well as an expert in nearly every other branch of forensic science. He told the court that the bullets removed from Phelps' body had been fired from Stielow's revolver; they could not have been fired from any other weapon, he declared. Stielow was convicted and sentenced to death.

His case was taken up by members of a penal reform society and several reprieves followed, one of them arriving after he had been strapped in the electric chair at Sing Sing Prison. A tramp named King confessed that he and his companion, both of whom were now serving prison sentences for other crimes, were guilty of the West Shelby murders — but retracted the confession after being taken away for questioning by Newton and Bartlett. By this time, however, the case was causing much disquiet, and Governor Whitman of New York appointed an independent commission to look into it.

During the course of their inquiry Stielow's revolver was examined by a New York City detective, Captain Jones, who said that it had not been fired for three or four years. When test shots were fired the bullets — unlike those from Phelps' body — were found to be covered with dirt from the barrel, and when the two sets of bullets were compared it was found that their markings were entirely different. It was then clear that Stielow was innocent, and eventually, after three years in jail, he was pardoned and set free.

Though King once more confessed to the murder of Phelps and his housekeeper — and there was evidence to show that he and his friend had known about the crime before it became general knowledge — a grand jury refused to indict him. The county's one serious crime in a whole generation was thus left officially unsolved, saving the cost of a fresh trial.

Murder of William Munday, 1905

On 23 March 1905, William Munday, an elderly gentleman, was held up by a tramp with a gun between Tooringa and Toowong, in Queensland. He resisted and was shot in the stomach, but managed to give a description of his attacker before dying in hospital the same evening. Later that night the tramp was arrested after trying unsuccessfully to draw a gun on the police officer concerned. The tramp was Robert Butler, a man with a long criminal record, who had spent most of his life in jail. He was charged with murder.

Butler, a native of Kilkenny, in Ireland, was an intelligent and literate man, but bitter and destructive. Arriving in Australia at the age of fourteen, he had spent thirteen of the next sixteen years in jail for crimes which included highway robbery and burglary. He then went to New Zealand, where he was given four years' hard labour for burglary, and later eighteen years' imprisonment, of which he served sixteen, for burning down the home of a solicitor. He was also tried for the murder of a young couple and their baby, but in this case he was acquitted; he had conducted his own defence.

Returning to Australia in 1896, he was given fifteen years, later reduced to ten, for burglary. At the same time he was acquitted on a charge of highway robbery, again after defending himself. He was released in 1904.

Brought to trial for the murder of Mr Munday, he was convicted and sentenced to death. While awaiting execution, he declared that he could not have the consolation of religion at his death, as there was 'an impassable bar' between himself and any religious organization. This incorrigible criminal was about sixty years old when the sentence was carried out.

About 7.30 a.m. on 27 March 1905, Thomas Farrow, an elderly tradesman, was found dead in the back parlour of his chandler's store in Deptford, south-east London; he had been battered over the head, and his body was covered with blood. His wife, Ann, was found unconscious in her bed upstairs, having been similarly attacked; she died in hospital three days later. The crime was discovered when a boy employed as an assistant in the store turned up for work.

It had taken place only half an hour earlier, the culprits knocking on the door of the shop and forcing their way in when Mr Farrow opened it. An empty cash-box, which had been broken open, showed that robbery had been the motive: it had earlier contained a few pounds. The main clues to the identities of those responsible were two black masks, made from silk stockings, and a thumbprint, in blood, on the cash-box tray. The masks suggested to the police that the crime had been committed by local men, afraid of being recognized.

The police questioned known criminals in the Deptford area and checked their alibis, and before long suspicion fell on Alfred Stratton, aged twenty-two, and his brother Albert, aged twenty, both of whom had convictions for house-breaking and burglary. Though both had disappeared, the police were able to speak to Alfred's girlfriend who had a black eye and was frightened. She informed them that the two brothers had both been out all night prior to the murder and that Alfred had afterwards destroyed his coat and dyed his brown shoes black.

On the Sunday following the murder a police officer found Alfred Stratton in a public house full of seamen, criminals and prostitutes; asking him to step outside, he promptly arrested him. Albert was found in a lodging-house in Stepney, and he, too, was arrested. Both were questioned and fingerprinted at Tower Bridge police station, and it was found that Alfred Stratton's right thumbprint matched the one found at the scene of the crime. They were charged with murder.

At their trial at the Old Bailey in May 1905, the thumb-print was an important part of the evidence, but its value was disputed by the defence. The jury, however, were impressed by a demonstration given by Inspector Collins of the newly-formed Finger-Print Branch at Scotland Yard and found both of the defendants guilty. Both blamed the other for the murders, and both were hanged. It was the first time that a conviction for murder had been obtained by fingerprint evidence in a British court.

Death of Mientje Manders, 1971

APRIL 2

On 2 April 1971, a girl named Mientje Manders died in Utrecht, Holland, after suffering from stomach pains for some days. It appeared that food poisoning was the cause of her death, but three months earlier another girl, Willy Maas, had also died in Utrecht after suffering from the same symptoms. Both girls had been engaged to a young man named Sjef Rijke, who was apparently grief-stricken on each occasion, but nonetheless married a third girl, eighteen-year-old Maria Haas, three weeks after the death of the second. Six weeks after that Rijke's wife left him and began divorce proceedings, having found him to be abnormally jealous.

Since the death of Mientje Manders the Utrecht police had been taking an interest in Rijke, and his wife was now interviewed. On being asked whether she had experienced any stomach pains, she revealed that she *had* had such pains from the time of her marriage but that they had stopped when she left her husband. Not long afterwards it was learnt that another girl, who had moved into Rijke's home in his wife's place, and begun to suffer similarly, had had a jar of peanut butter analysed at the local health department's laboratory where it was found to contain rat poison.

Even so, the police were not certain that Rijke was responsible, for he seemed to have no motive for poisoning any of these girls: they therefore arrested his middle-aged cleaning woman as well as him, releasing the cleaner only when a local store-owner informed them that Rijke had bought rat poison from him on a number of occasions.

Rijke then admitted that he had been responsible for the deaths of Willy Maas and Mientje Manders, and also that he had poisoned his wife and the girl who had lived with him after his wife had left. He denied that he had intended to murder anyone, saying that the poisonings had only taken place because he enjoyed watching women suffer.

Brought to trial in January 1972, Sjef Rijke was convicted of the murders of Willy Maas and Mientje Manders and sentenced to life imprisonment for each crime.

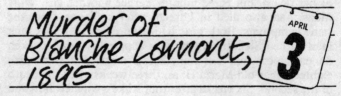

Murder of Blanche Lamont, 1895

APRIL 3

On 3 April 1895, Blanche Lamont, a twenty-one-year-old student teacher and regular church-goer, was murdered in

San Francisco's Bartlett Street Emmanuel Baptist Church, where her body lay in the belfry for the next eleven days. Before its discovery Miss Lamont's friend Marion Williams, known as 'Minnie', was also killed in the same building. It was the body of Miss Williams, whose murder had taken place on 12 April, which was found first.

Blanche Lamont, who lived with her uncle and aunt, Mr and Mrs Noble, had been seen entering the church in the company of William Durrant, a twenty-four-year-old medical student and church official, on the afternoon of her death. Durrant afterwards offered to help Mrs Noble to find her, but cautioned her against telling others about the girl's disappearance. Three rings belonging to Miss Lamont were received by her aunt on the morning of 13 April, having been sent through the post anonymously.

Minnie Williams left a friend's house to go to church about eight o'clock on the evening of 12 April. The following morning the new pastor, J. George Gibson, reported finding that a door of the church had been forced, and later a female volunteer worker found Miss Williams' body in the library; she had been strangled, then mutilated with a table-knife. It was afterwards alleged that the police were not informed of this discovery until after Gibson had made an unsuccessful attempt to get the body removed secretly by a local undertaker.

On 14 April a patrolman on duty at the church climbed to the belfry and found the naked body of Blanche Lamont, who lay with her hands crossed on her breasts. She, too, had been strangled, but not mutilated, and nobody doubted that the two murders had been committed by the same person.

Durrant was arrested and brought to trial on 22 July. The case lasted until 1 November, but the jury took only twenty minutes to find him guilty of first-degree murder; he was sentenced to death. The trial received much publicity, the 'Demon in the Belfry' making news in Europe as well as the United States. After four stays of execution, he was hanged at San Quentin Prison on 7

January, 1898, protesting his innocence to the end.

The execution was followed by a number of false confessions, and the idea that Gibson rather than Durrant had murdered the two girls gained a certain amount of support.

Horrifying murder in Barking, 1968

APRIL 4

On the morning of 4 April, 1968, Suchnam Singh Sandhu, a thirty-nine-year-old Punjab Sikh living in Barking, Essex, murdered his teenage daughter Sarabjit in a horrifying manner. Sarabjit, who lived away from home, had been staying with her family for a few days and had been left in her father's company while her mother was out and her two younger sisters were at school. Following a bitter argument — over a married man living in India — Sarabjit told her father that she had taken poison and written a letter blaming him for her impending death. Suchnam Singh, who was still in his pyjamas, then lost his temper and struck her twice with a hammer.

Having done so, he dressed quickly and went out, returning to the house half an hour later with a high-tensile hacksaw which he had just bought for the purpose of dismembering his daughter's body. Sarabjit, at this stage, was not dead and when he started to cut her neck she tried to grasp the saw, cutting her thumb in the attempt. But Suchnam Singh, now wearing his pyjamas again, went on sawing until he had cut off her head, then cut through her body at the waist and severed her legs at the knees. The dismemberment was carried out with the body in a large plastic bag, so that Sarabjit's blood could afterwards be poured into the bath.

With this frightful task accomplished, Suchnam Singh put the upper part of his daughter's body into one suitcase, the lower part, together with the severed legs, into another, and her head into a duffel bag, ready for disposal. The blood-stained pyjamas and the hacksaw were put into his dustbin.

That night the first suitcase was taken by public transport to Euston Station, London, where it was placed on the 10.40 p.m. train to Wolverhampton; the other was thrown into the River Roding from a bridge at Ilford. The following morning — by which time the first suitcase had been opened at Wolverhampton — the duffel bag was left near a roadside on Wanstead Flats, in Essex.

After the discovery of part of Sarabjit's remains, the police made a public appeal for information about a young Asian woman who might recently have left home or disappeared from a boarding-house. They later issued a photofit picture of a coloured man whom a ticket-collector at Euston remembered seeing with a suitcase before the departure of the Wolverhampton train.

When the second suitcase was found, also on 5 April, it was quickly established that the contents of both were parts of the same body. From an examination of the stomach contents it was learnt that the young woman had taken a fatal dose of phenobarbitone but that she had died before this had been absorbed into her system. It also appeared, from a scar on the inside of one of her legs and the fact that her pubic hair had been shaved off three or four months earlier, that she had received gynaecological treatment.

Detectives then began checking on Indian and Pakistani women who had received such treatment, and eventually the corpse — the head of which was discovered by a cyclist on 8 May — was identified by a doctor whom Sarabjit had been to see in Ilford in November 1967. Sarabjit, who had been pregnant at the time, had been sent to a consultant gynaecologist at Barking Hospital, where she had afterwards failed to keep an appointment for ante-natal treatment. It appeared that she had had an abortion during the next few weeks, though the police never discovered who had performed it.

On 11 May Suchnam Singh, a machine-minder, was questioned by police about his missing daughter. He said that Sarabjit had left home in February 1968, and that he did not know her whereabouts. He also denied knowing that she had been pregnant and refused to identify the suit-cases or items of clothing found with her remains. Two days later, however, he made a full confession. He was then charged with murder.

Sarabjit, it was learnt, had been Suchnam Singh's favourite child, and he — an educated man who had formerly been a schoolmaster — had wanted her to become a doctor. But then she had become pregnant, thus bringing the family into disgrace, and had further angered her father by saying that she was in love with a man who was already married, and wanted him to divorce or kill his wife so that he could marry her.

At the time of the murder Suchnam Singh, having struck his daughter with the hammer, had done his best to follow an old Sikh custom — that of dismembering one who had disgraced the family and sending parts of the body on trains going in different directions.

He was later brought to trial at the Old Bailey, where the evidence against him was shown to be overwhelming, and after retiring for ninety minutes the jury found him guilty of murder. He was sent to prison for life.

Jeanne Weber suspected of attempted murder, 1905

APRIL
5

On the afternoon of 5 April 1905, Maurice Weber, aged six months, was taken to the Bretonneau Hospital in Paris suffering from acute asphyxia. He had been left in the care of an aunt, Jeanne Weber, who lived in a slum in the Passage Goutte d'Or, and shortly afterwards had been found blue in the face and choking. Jeanne Weber, aged thirty, had been sitting beside him with her hands under his vest.

The resident physician examined the child and found a reddish mark on his neck which made the doctor suspect that an attempt had been made to choke him. Later, when the child had recovered, the doctor questioned the mother at length and learnt of the deaths of four other children, all related, in the previous few weeks. All had died mysteriously after being left in Jeanne Weber's charge.

The first had been Georgette Weber, a niece aged eighteen months, who had died on 2 March while her mother was working in the public laundry; the cause had been diagnosed as 'convulsions'. Georgette's sister Suzanne, a year older, had died in similar circumstances on 11 March; her death had also been put down to 'convulsions'. On 26 March a third niece, Germaine Weber, seven-month-old daughter of another brother-in-law, had died while her mother was out shopping, and this, too, had been put down to the same cause. Finally, on 27 March, the day on which Germaine was buried, Jeanne Weber's own seven-year-old son, Marcel, had fallen ill and died, the diagnosis in this case being diphtheria.

The doctor found all this information disturbing. The following morning, after examining the child again, he consulted the doctor in charge of the children's ward, who made his own examination and came to the same conclusion. As a result, the police were informed and Jeanne Weber taken into custody. It was then discovered that she had had two other children besides Marcel, both of whom had died, and that two others had died while in her care in 1902.

The interviewing of witnesses produced other startling pieces of information. On the day that Georgette died the child's mother had been called away from the laundry by a neighbour, who had entered the apartment after hearing screams; she had arrived home to find Georgette's tongue hanging out and foam on her lips, but had then gone back to the laundry after holding her in front of an open window for a while. A similar thing had happened *twice* on consecutive days before Germaine's death, except that in this case a doctor had been called each time.

Though Dr Léon Thoinot, the pathologist appointed to examine the exhumed bodies of the four children, found no signs of strangulation or choking, the examining magistrate was convinced of Jeanne Weber's guilt and determined to have her brought to trial. But when the trial took place, in January 1906, Thoinot's evidence proved to be devastating and the accused was acquitted. Soon afterwards she disappeared.

The following year, using a different name, she appeared in the village of Chambon, near Villedieu, where she became the housekeeper and mistress of a peasant named Bavouzet, who had three children. A few weeks later one of the children, a boy of nine, died suddenly, his death being put down to 'convulsions resulting from an irritation of the meninges'. The case was investigated when Jeanne Weber's identity was discovered; the child was then found to have died of strangulation. Jeanne Weber was arrested and brought to trial again, but with the same result as before.

The year after that she arrived in Commercy with a lime-burner named Émile Bouchery, who introduced her as his wife. The couple rented a room at an inn, but Bouchery had to go out that evening and said he would return late at night; the innkeeper and his wife therefore allowed their seven-year-old son to sleep in the room, to keep Jeanne company. They were later summoned by another lodger who had heard the child screaming.

Breaking into the room, the innkeeper and his wife found their son lying on the bed with his face discoloured and blood streaming from his mouth. Jeanne Weber lay beside him, her hands and her petticoat bloodstained. The boy died soon afterwards, his death having been caused by strangulation. The bleeding had been caused by his biting his tongue.

When the case was reported in the newspapers there was a storm of indignation. Jeanne Weber, however, was not brought to trial this time; instead, she was declared insane and committed to a mental hospital. She remained there until she committed suicide two years later.

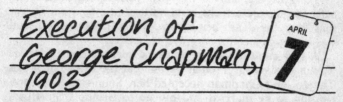

Execution of George Chapman, 1903

APRIL 7

George Chapman, who was hanged on 7 April 1903, was a philanderer and bigamist who poisoned three women with antimony, probably because he had grown tired of them. It has been suggested that he was also responsible for the 'Jack the Ripper' murders.

Chapman was a native of Poland, his real name being Severin Antoniovitch Klosovski. The son of a carpenter, he had been apprenticed to a surgeon at the age of fifteen, but failed to get a degree. After his arrival in London in 1888 he worked as a barber's assistant in the East End.

He was already married by this time, but had left his wife in Poland. Later, when she joined him in England, she found him living with another Polish woman, Lucy Baderski, whom he had also married. The two women lived in the same house with him for a short while, until the legal wife left.

Klosovski and Lucy Baderski went to America together in 1890, but parted company the following year, Klosovski coming back to England in 1892. He changed his name to George Chapman after living for a year with a girl named Annie Chapman.

In 1895 he took up with a married woman, Mary Spink, who had been deserted by her husband. They lived together, claiming to be married, and Mrs Spink — who had private means — allowed him to use some of her money to open a hairdressing shop in Hastings in 1897.

Though this proved popular, with Mrs Spink playing the piano for the benefit of customers, they gave it up six months later and moved back to London, taking the lease of the Prince of Wales Tavern, off City Road.

Towards the end of the year Mrs Spink became ill, suffering severe attacks of vomiting. She died on Christmas Day, her death being put down to consumption, and was buried in a common grave at Leyton.

A few months later a domestic servant named Bessie Taylor applied for a job as barmaid at the Prince of Wales Tavern, and Chapman accepted her. Soon they were pretending to be married and moved to Bishop's Stortford, but then returned to London, where Chapman set himself up in the Monument Tavern, in Borough.

Bessie's health was deteriorating by this time and Chapman treated her violently. When she died, in February 1901, 'exhaustion from vomiting and diarrhoea' was stated to be the cause.

After another few months Chapman met Maud Marsh, whom he also employed as a barmaid. The daughter of a labourer in Croydon, she soon became his mistress, though only after he had threatened to dismiss her. They began to live as man and wife not long afterwards.

The following year, 1902, they moved to a new pub, the Crown, which was in the same road as the Monument Tavern. Maud had also begun to suffer from vomiting and diarrhoea and, although she recovered in hospital, she became ill again after being discharged.

Her mother, who was nursing her, became ill herself after drinking a glass of brandy and soda which Chapman had prepared for Maud. This made her suspicious enough to ask her own doctor to examine Maud, and he, having done so, warned Chapman's doctor that she was being poisoned. When Maud died, on 22 October 1902, Chapman's doctor refused to issue a death certificate.

Chapman was arrested three days later and charged with her murder; he was later charged with the murders of Mary Spink and Bessie Taylor, too. His trial began at the Old Bailey on 16 March 1903, and lasted four days. He was hanged at Wandsworth Prison, at the age of thirty-seven.

Superintendent of Milford Sanatorium poisoned, 1949

APRIL 9

During the late afternoon of 9 April 1949, the superintendent of the Milford Sanatorium at Godalming, in Surrey, found a brown-paper parcel containing part of a fruit pie in his office. His secretary was not there, as it was Saturday, and there was no message to tell him who had sent it. He therefore assumed that it was from one of his friends and, taking it home with him, started to eat it. Before long he was seized with pain and began to be violently sick.

He spent the rest of the weekend in bed, feeling very ill and unable to eat anything else, and on Monday, when he returned to work, he was still weak and suffering from a stomach ache. He was then given a letter which had been left in his secretary's in-tray two days earlier. It was from a Mrs Formby, and explained the arrival of the fruit pie, which the superintendent already suspected to have been the cause of his illness.

Mrs Formby was a friend of Mrs Margery Radford, an inmate of the sanatorium, who had received the pie from her husband and been ill herself after eating some of it. Fearing it to be poisoned, she had asked Mrs Formby to have its contents analysed, informing her that she had been ill on several other occasions after receiving food or drink sent by her husband. But Mrs Formby, after consulting her own husband, had decided not to send it to Scotland Yard, as her friend had requested, but to the superintendent instead.

Having read the letter and spoken to Margery Radford, who was now close to death, the superintendent called the Surrey police. The following day the remains of the fruit pie were sent to the laboratories at Scotland Yard, where they were found to contain arsenic. Margery Radford, having suffered from tuberculosis for seven years, died on the very day that this discovery was made. It was then found that she had been systematically poisoned over a period of three months.

Her husband, Frederick Gordon Radford, was a laboratory technician at a hospital about a mile from the sanatorium. He had not been attentive to his ailing wife and was believed to have a mistress; the pies and mineral drinks which Mrs Radford had received, though bought by her husband, were delivered by her father, a Mr Kite. On being told that arsenic had been found in one of the pies and also in his wife's body, Radford held his face in his hands, denying all knowledge of the matter.

'Why should I want to kill my wife?' he asked. 'I knew she was going to die anyway. I would not be such a fool as to use arsenic with my experience, as I know the police could find it easily enough.' He then challenged Detective Superintendent Roberts, head of the Surrey CID, to charge him 'and let a judge and jury decide'.

Superintendent Roberts was not yet ready to make an arrest, as it was just possible that the suspect was telling the truth. Frederick Radford was therefore driven home by police officers after agreeing to attend the inquest the following day. In the morning, however, he was found dead, his body already cold. He had poisoned himself with cyanide.

Murder of David Blakely, 1955

APRIL
10

On the night of 10 April 1955, Ruth Ellis, a twenty-eight-year-old divorcée and night-club hostess, peered through a window of a public house in Hampstead, London, and saw her former lover inside. She waited outside for him, and when he emerged she produced a gun and fired at him six times in quick succession. David Blakely, a twenty-five-year-old racing driver, was killed instantly, and a passer-by was wounded in the hand.

Ruth Ellis was immediately apprehended and taken to Hampstead police station, where she admitted the shooting. 'I am guilty,' she said, adding: 'I am rather confused.' At her trial at the Old Bailey in June she was asked what her intention had been when she fired the shots. 'I intended to kill him,' she replied.

Blakely and Ruth Ellis had been lovers for the previous two years, and a few weeks earlier had set up home together in Egerton Gardens, Kensington. However, neither of them had been faithful to the other and both had resented the other's affairs. After many bitter quarrels, Blakely left without telling her where he was going. At the beginning of April she had a miscarriage.

On Good Friday — 8 April — she tried to see him at a house in Tanza Road, Hampstead, where she knew that he was spending Easter in the company of friends. But he refused to see her, and when she became noisy the police were called. It was from the same house that Blakely went out to the pub on the evening of 10 April.

Ruth Ellis was convicted and sentenced to death. Despite many petitions for a commutation, she was hanged at Holloway Prison on 13 July 1955, the execution causing much astonishment and disgust. It was the last time that a woman was hanged in Britain.

In July 1983, Ruth's daughter, then aged thirty-one, gave a newspaper interview to the *Sunday Mirror*, in which she spoke of the anguish which she had suffered as a result of knowing that her mother had been hanged.

'For most of my life I have tried to face up to the image of the hangman peering through the peephole into her cell, trying to work out how much rope he should use to make sure that frail little neck was broken,' she said. 'As for the scene on the gallows, I just blank it out.'

Her half-brother, born in 1944, had had similar problems, though he had been brought up separately. He took his own life in 1982, after years of depression.

Beginning of Adelaide Bartlett's trial, 1886

APRIL
12

On 12 April 1886, the trial of Adelaide Bartlett, aged thirty, for the murder of her husband, began at the Old Bailey. Edwin Bartlett, a forty-year-old grocer, had been found dead at the couple's lodgings in the Pimlico district of London on 1 January the same year. He had died as a result of taking a large dose of liquid chloroform.

The accused was the illegitimate daughter of a well-born Frenchwoman; she had been brought up in France and had come to England to complete her education. Her marriage had taken place in 1875.

Edwin Bartlett was an ambitious businessman and a staunch Wesleyan. Though good-humoured, he gave his wife less attention than she would have liked, with the result that she was often bored. For a period of five years her father-in-law lived with them, her husband having invited him to do so without consulting her. However, they gave the impression of being a contented couple.

In 1885 they became acquainted with a young Wesleyan minister, the Reverend George Dyson, who visited them frequently. Dyson and Adelaide were attracted to each other and began to have an affair — with Bartlett's knowledge and approval. Bartlett made a will, leaving everything to his wife and naming her lover as the executor. He also made it clear that he wanted Dyson to have Adelaide in the event of his own death.

In December Bartlett was seriously ill, but recovered well enough to celebrate Christmas. On the day before his death he visited his dentist and appeared to be in good health. It was afterwards revealed that on 29 December Dyson had given Adelaide a large amount of chloroform which he had bought in small amounts from three different chemists.

Though Dyson had also been charged with the murder, no evidence was offered against him when the case came to court. Adelaide claimed that she used chloroform in order to resist her husband's sexual demands — by getting him to inhale it. As no traces of it were found in the dead man's mouth or windpipe, the jury, at the end of the six-day trial, concluded that while grave suspicion attached to the defendant, there was insufficient evidence to show how or by whom the chloroform had been administered. She was therefore acquitted.

A study of the case by Yseult Bridges, entitled *Poison and Adelaide Bartlett,* puts forward the theory that Edwin Bartlett was induced to drink the chloroform while under the influence of hypnotic suggestion.

Death of Sarah Ricketts, 1953

On 14 April 1953, Sarah Ricketts, a seventy-nine-year-old widow of Devonshire Road, Blackpool, died of phosphorus poisoning, her death occurring at 3.15 a.m. in the presence of Louisa Merrifield, her housekeeper. Mrs Merrifield, aged forty-six, did not call in a doctor until nearly eleven hours later, but tried unsuccessfully to get an undertaker to cremate the body 'at once'. Later, when the bungalow and garden were being searched by police, she made arrangements for members of the Salvation Army to play *Abide With Me* outside.

Louisa Merrifield and her third husband Alfred, aged seventy-one, had moved into Mrs Ricketts' home only a few weeks earlier, Mrs Merrifield having obtained the job after seeing it advertised in a newspaper. Mrs Merrifield had had twenty similar jobs in the previous three years; she also had a criminal record, having served a prison sentence for ration-book frauds. Mrs Ricketts, despite feeling that she was not being properly looked after — she complained that she was not given enough food — had since changed her will in the couple's favour.

'We are landed', Mrs Merrifield told an acquaintance a few days before Mrs Ricketts' death. 'We went living with an old lady and she died and left me a bungalow worth £4000.' When asked which old lady she was talking about, she replied, 'She's not dead yet, but she soon will be'.

During a medical examination on the day before her death Mrs Ricketts was found to be in reasonably good health.

The search of the bungalow failed to reveal any trace of the poison, but a substance attached to a teaspoon in Mrs Merrifield's handbag was found to be the residue which resulted from phosphorus being mixed with rum. Alfred Merrifield was identified by a Blackpool chemist's assistant from whom he had purchased a tin of rat poison which contained phosphorus.

Louisa and Alfred Merrifield were brought to trial in Manchester in July, both pleading not guilty to the murder; the case lasted eleven days. Louisa stated that she had found Mrs Ricketts on the floor of her bedroom at 3.15 a.m. on the day of her death, and went on to tell the court: 'I picked her up and put her into bed. She said she was thankful to me. Those were the last words she spoke.' On being asked why she had not immediately gone for help, she replied, 'Well, it was not such a nice time in the morning to go out on the streets and call a doctor.'

Though the defence contended that Mrs Ricketts had died from cirrhosis of the liver, the jury found Louisa Merrifield guilty of murder and she was sentenced to death. In the case of her husband they were unable to reach agreement; the judge therefore ordered that he should be retried at the following assizes, but the case against him was finally dropped. Louisa Merrifield was hanged at Manchester's Strangeways Prison on 18 September 1953.

Alfred Merrifield, on being released, received his half-share of Mrs Ricketts' bungalow, and later appeared in sideshows in Blackpool. He died, aged eighty, in 1962.

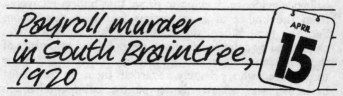

Payroll murder in South Braintree, 1920

APRIL 15

On the afternoon of 15 April 1920, two employees of the Slater and Morrill Shoe Company were shot and fatally wounded by two other men while delivering the $16,000 weekly payroll to the company's factory in South Braintree, Massachusetts. The two killers, having grabbed the money, escaped in a car with a third gunman who had taken no active part in the crime; another two men were also seen in the car with them. The two victims were Frederick A. Parmenter, the paymaster, and Alexander Berardelli, an armed guard.

The two men who had fired the shots were both described as 'foreign-looking', one of them being clean-shaven and the other having a moustache. It was as a result of these descriptions that a police officer boarded a streetcar in the same district on 5 May and arrested two Italian immigrants, Nicola Sacco, a shoemaker aged twenty-nine, and Bartolomeo Vanzetti, a fish-pedlar aged thirty-two. Both were found to be armed with guns, Sacco having a .32 Colt automatic and Venzetti a .38 revolver; both were also found to be anarchists.

Though each was initially charged with possessing a firearm without a permit, Sacco was later brought to trial for taking part in an attempted payroll robbery in Bridgewater, near Boston, the previous Christmas. On being convicted of this offence, he was sentenced to ten to fifteen years' imprisonment. By this time he and Vanzetti had been charged with the South Braintree murders.

Their trial, which began in Dedham, Massachusetts, on 31 May 1921, made headline news in many countries. Some sixty witnesses appeared for the prosecution, and nearly 100 for the defence. The prosecution produced ballistics evidence, seeking to prove that bullets recovered from the bodies of both victims had been fired from Sacco's gun. While the value of this evidence was challenged by defence witnesses, the political sympathies of the defendants made bias inevitable. The conduct of the trial judge, who privately regarded them as 'anarchist bastards', was afterwards to be the subject of much criticism. Sacco and Vanzetti were both found guilty of first-degree murder and sentenced to death.

There were immediate demands for another trial. Organizations were set up to raise funds for their defence and a campaign of agitation began. During the next six years many petitions for clemency were presented and many protests staged. In legal circles disquiet was expressed at the verdict and the means by which it had been reached. But, on 9 April 1927, after no fewer than seven motions for a new trial had been heard and dismissed, the death sentences were confirmed. Sacco and Vanzetti were executed in the electric chair on 23 August 1927.

The controversy to which the case had given rise continued long after their deaths, and has never been forgotten. In 1977 their names were cleared in a special proclamation issued by the Governor of Massachusetts.

Six killed in Glasgow arson attack, 1984

APRIL 16

During the early hours of 16 April 1984, an arson attack was made on a Glasgow council flat, resulting in the deaths of six people. The flat, which was the home of a family named Doyle, was on the top floor of a block in Backend Street, Ruchazie. As the front door was its only exit, and petrol had been poured through the letter-box and ignited, the people inside were trapped. One of the survivors, twenty-one-year-old Stephen Doyle, only managed to escape the blaze by jumping fifty feet to the concrete below, injuring his back and legs in the process.

Stephen's brother Anthony, aged fourteen, and his twenty-five-year-old sister, Mrs Christine Halleron, both died in the flames; his father, James Doyle, aged fifty-

113

three, his brothers James and Andrew, aged twenty-three and eighteen respectively, and Mrs Halleron's eighteen-month-old son Mark all died later. James Doyle's grief-stricken widow Lilian, aged fifty-two, who was rescued by firemen after perching on a window-ledge, said later that she wished that she, too, had died in the fire which claimed the lives of her husband, sons, daughter and grandson.

The attack had been the work of Thomas Campbell, a thirty-one-year-old gangster determined to take control of Glasgow's lucrative ice-cream trade, and one of his henchmen, a twenty-two-year-old petty thief named Joseph Steele. Campbell, who had already served a ten-year prison sentence, had been responsible for many attacks on drivers working for Marchetti Brothers, a well-established rival company, and was believed to have taken part in an attempt to burn down that company's premises.

Andrew Doyle, one of the drivers concerned, had actually been hired by Marchetti Brothers to protect two of their other vans rather than sell ice-cream. On one occasion he had been threatened and his van had been damaged with pickaxe handles; on another a man with a shotgun had fired through his windscreen. Then, a week after the second attack, a group of men had beaten him up in the street. But Andrew Doyle had refused to be intimidated by Campbell's men. It was because of this that the arson attack had taken place.

Though the police officers investigating the crime had little difficulty finding out what had happened, they hesitated to make arrests for fear that they would prove to be premature. A twenty-four-year-old man, William Love, was charged in connection with the shotgun attack and, while denying that he had committed the offence, agreed that he had been at the scene on the day in question; he afterwards made a statement claiming to have overheard Campbell and others planning to set fire to the Doyles' front door, as 'a frightener'. However, it was 12 May before the police took Campbell into custody and 1 June before they arrested Joseph Steele.

Eventually, on 3 September 1984, the case described as 'Scotland's biggest multiple murder trial' began in Glasgow, with Campbell, Steele and five other men appearing, each charged with offences in connection with the gang's activities. It lasted twenty-seven days, with one of the accused being released when the prosecution withdrew charges against him, and others being cleared on some charges because the judge found insufficient evidence against them.

But at the end of the trial Thomas Campbell and Joseph Steele were both given sentences of life imprisonment for murdering the six members of the Doyle family, the judge recommending that Campbell should serve twenty years, but making no recommendation in Steele's case. Campbell was also given ten years, to run concurrently, for taking part in the shotgun attack, and Steele received two shorter sentences, also to run concurrently, for conspiracy and damaging an ice-cream van.

Of the other accused, Thomas Gray, aged thirty-one, was sentenced to fourteen years for attempted murder; Thomas Lafferty, forty, was given three years for taking part in the shotgun attack; George Reid, thirty-three, received a total of three years for a knife assault and for damaging an ice-cream van, and John Campbell, twenty-one, was given a year for taking part in the attack on the ice-cream van and three years for taking part in the shotgun attack.

The jailing of Campbell and his fellow-accused did not bring Glasgow's 'ice-cream war' to an end, for others associated with them have continued to operate vans on the city's council estates and many further cases of assault and damage have been reported by drivers working for Marchetti Brothers. It is believed that, in spite of the length of his sentence, Campbell is still directing the activities of gang members who were not arrested from his prison cell.

On 18 April 1912, Frederick Seddon, a forty-year-old
insurance agent, was hanged at Pentonville Prison for the
murder of Eliza Barrow, a lodger at his three-storey house
in Tollington Park, north London. Miss Barrow, aged
forty-nine, had died from arsenic poisoning on 14 September previously.

Seddon was a mean and calculating man, obsessed with
making and saving money. He had worked for the same
insurance company for over twenty years, but was
constantly dealing in other things — anything which
enabled him to make a profit, in fact — and even managed
to make 2s 6d (12$\frac{1}{2}$p) commission out of his victim's
funeral. He owned various properties in addition to the
house at Tollington Park, where he and his family occupied
the lower floors. His crime, needless to say, was committed
for gain.

Eliza Barrow, who had moved into the house in July
1910, was shabby and dirty, and every bit as miserly as
Seddon himself. She occupied the top floor, and had an
orphan boy, the son of an earlier landlord and landlady,
living with her.

At the beginning of her tenancy she had both property
and money, but gradually her fortune passed into Seddon's
hands, as she was impressed by his financial astuteness and
thought he was helping her to take care of it. After her
death he took over £400 in gold coins from her cash-box,
and then arranged a pauper's burial for her, haggling with
the undertaker over the cost of it.

Eliza Barrow's doctor, without seeing the body, made
out a death certificate, giving the cause as 'epidemic diarrhoea'. But after complaints from her relatives, who were

116

suspicious of Seddon's evasive answers to their questions, an exhumation was authorized and a post-mortem carried out. On 4 December Seddon was arrested and charged with murder. His wife was similarly charged a few weeks later.

Frederick and Margaret Seddon were brought to trial at the Old Bailey on 4 March 1912, both pleading not guilty. The case lasted ten days, three of them being taken up by Seddon's own evidence; this was given in such an arrogant and self-assured manner that it served only to antagonize everyone. So, while his wife was acquitted, Seddon — against whom the case was no stronger — was convicted. When asked if he had anything to say before sentence was passed, he made a long speech protesting his innocence, during the course of which he raised his hand as though taking an oath of freemasonry.

The judge, who, like Seddon, was a freemason, said in reply: 'You and I know we belong to one brotherhood ... But our brotherhood does not encourage crime; on the contrary, it condemns it. I pray you again to make your peace with the Great Architect of the Universe. Mercy — pray for it, ask for it'. He was in tears as he pronounced sentence.

Seddon was the father of five children, the youngest of which had been born just a few months before the murder. Margaret Seddon remarried and moved to Liverpool a few months after her husband's execution. She made herself a lot of money out of a newspaper confession, stating that she had seen Frederick Seddon giving poison to Eliza Barrow on the night before her death. However, she published a second statement a fortnight afterwards, claiming that the first had been a lie. Eventually she emigrated to America.

Trial of David Greenwood, 1918

APRIL 24

On 24 April 1918, David Greenwood, a twenty-one-year-old turner, was brought to trial at the Old Bailey, charged with the murder of Nellie Trew, aged sixteen, on 9 February previously. He denied the offence.

On the day of the murder the victim, a junior clerk working at Woolwich Arsenal, had left her home at Juno Terrace, Eltham Well Hall, to change a book at Plumstead Library. The following morning she was found raped and strangled on Eltham Common, about a quarter of a mile away. Her father had reported her missing when she failed to return home by midnight.

A replica of the badge of the Leicestershire Regiment and an overcoat button, which had been threaded with a piece of wire, were found trodden into the mud near the scene of the crime. The police had a photograph of both articles published in all the popular newspapers on the day after the body had been found.

David Greenwood, who worked for the Hewson Manufacturing Company near Oxford Street, normally wore a badge on the lapel of his overcoat. One of his workmates noticed that it was missing and remarked, pointing to the newspaper photograph, 'That looks uncommonly like the badge you were wearing.' Greenwood agreed, explaining that he had sold his badge two days earlier to a man he had met on a tram. It was then suggested to him that he should go to the police and 'clear the matter up'.

The same day, at lunch time, Greenwood went to the police station in Tottenham Court Road and told the same story. The police, learning that he lived in Eltham, took a particular interest in him, and the next day an inspector went to his place of work and took him back to Scotland Yard.

118

It was noticed that all the buttons had been removed from his overcoat, and that there was a little tear where one of them had been. The piece of wire which had been attached to the button discovered on Eltham Common was found to be part of a spring; the same type of spring was used at the Hewson works.

At his trial Greenwood's war record was revealed. Having enlisted at the beginning of the First World War, he had fought in the trenches and been buried alive at Ypres. He had then been discharged, suffering from neurasthenia, shell-shock and a weak heart. The defence suggested that he was not physically capable of committing the crime of which he stood accused.

The jury found the defendant guilty, adding a recommendation of mercy. His death sentence was commuted just before he was due to be executed, and he spent the next fifteen years in prison. At his release, in 1933, he was thirty-six years old.

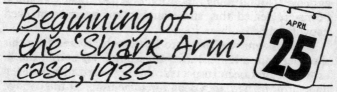

Beginning of the 'Shark Arm' case, 1935

APRIL 25

On 25 April 1935, a shark in an Australian aquarium began to vomit and, to the disgust of spectators, brought up a man's arm. When this was removed from the pool by police it was found to be so well preserved that a tattoo depicting two boxers was clearly visible on it. As there was also a length of rope tied tightly round the wrist, the police immediately suspected that a murder or suicide had taken place.

The shark had been caught by two fishermen off the beaches near Sydney a week earlier, when it became entangled in their lines. Not knowing what else to do with it, they had given it to the Coogee Beach aquarium. But it had not taken to captivity and its digestive system had failed to function normally. It died shortly afterwards.

No trace of any other part of the man's body was found in the shark's stomach or intestines, so an extensive search of the beaches and sea-bed was started in the area in which it had been caught. Though this was to be in vain, a study of missing-persons lists led to the man's identification. He was found to be James Smith, a forty-year-old former boxer who had worked as a marker in a billiard hall owned by Reginald Holmes, a wealthy boat-builder, prior to his disappearance. His wife and brother both identified the arm from its tattoo marks.

Smith had left his home on 8 April, telling his wife that he was going on a fishing holiday with a man named Patrick Brady, and that they would be staying in a rented cottage on the coast; she had heard nothing from him since. The police already knew Brady, a forty-two-year-old forger, and though he denied all knowledge of Smith's death, he was taken into custody. He then accused Smith's employer of dealing in forgeries. Reginald Holmes, however, denied this and claimed that he did not even know Brady.

Smith's arm was found to have been severed from his shoulder with a knife, rather than bitten off by the shark, as had at first been suspected; this appeared to have been done after he had been dead for some time. At the cottage on the coast a tin trunk, a mattress, three mats and a length of rope were found to be missing. It was therefore supposed that the body had been cut up there and pushed into the trunk, those parts for which there was insufficient room being tied to the outside. The trunk had then been taken out to sea and dumped, together with the mattress and mats, which were presumably bloodstained.

Three days after Brady's arrest Reginald Holmes, steering his speedboat in an erratic manner in Sydney Harbour, was pursued by a police launch. When the police caught up with him after a four-hour chase he was found to be suffering from a superficial bullet wound in his head and claimed that somebody had tried to kill him. He then admitted knowing Brady, and accused him of killing Smith and disposing of the body. On 17 May Brady was charged with murder.

However, on the night before the coroner's inquest Holmes, by now the most important witness, was shot dead in his car under Sydney Harbour Bridge, the sound of the shot being drowned by the noise of overhead traffic. Brady's lawyers then obtained an order from the Supreme Court to stop the inquest — after forty witnesses had been heard — on the grounds that Smith's severed arm was no proof of his death. Brady was released on bail, and at his trial in September for Smith's murder was acquitted for lack of evidence.

It was understood that both Smith and Brady had been involved in drug-trafficking and underworld intimidation, and that Holmes had been murdered in order to ensure his silence. But Brady, who died in 1965, maintained his innocence of Smith's murder to the end, and two other men who were tried for Holmes' murder were both acquitted.

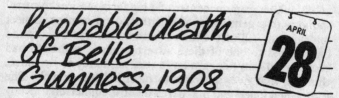

Probable death of Belle Gunness, 1908

APRIL 28

On 28 April 1908, a farm on the outskirts of La Porte, in Indiana, owned by a widow named Belle Gunness, was burnt to the ground. The fire, which had been started deliberately, led to the discovery of four bodies among the debris, and fourteen others which had been dismembered and buried. The four recovered from the debris were believed to be those of the widow and her three children. The other fourteen were found to be the remains of men who had been murdered by the widow for their money.

Belle Gunness, who was born in Norway in 1859, had had two husbands, both of whom had died; the death of the second had occurred in suspicious circumstances in La Porte in 1904. She had since managed the farm with the help of a local handyman, Ray Lamphere, who was also her lover. It was believed that Lamphere had killed her and then set fire to the farm in order to prevent the crime being discovered. However, the body believed to be hers was inexplicably headless. Those involved in the investigation had to point to the finding of her denture in order to prove that it *was* hers.

Almost immediately after Lamphere's arrest a stranger arrived in La Porte in search of his missing brother. Andrew Hegelein, of South Dakota, was known to have visited the farm, taking $1000 in cash, but nothing had been heard from him since; his brother, having written to Mrs Gunness, had now come to see her about it. Before long it was discovered that Andrew Hegelein was one of the men who had been murdered.

Mrs Gunness was found to have been in the practice of placing newspaper advertisements in other parts of America, each of them worded in the same way: 'Rich, good-looking woman, owner of a big farm, desires to correspond with a gentleman of wealth and refinement. Object matrimony.' All of the men whose bodies had been found had replied to one of these advertisements, and each had been duped into taking a large sum of money to the farm, thinking that he was about to meet his future wife. The widow had killed and butchered all of them herself.

Ray Lamphere was brought to trial for the widow's murder, but acquitted. At the same time, however, he was convicted of setting fire to her property and given a sentence of two to twenty-one years' imprisonment. He died of tuberculosis in the Indiana State Penitentiary.

He had, at some stage, made a claim that the widow's death had been faked, the headless corpse found after the fire being that of a drunken female tramp from Chicago. But, while this might explain why the head was missing, it also suggests that Mrs Gunness was responsible for the deaths of her own children, of whom she was very fond. It is therefore unlikely to be true.

Arrest of Patrick Mahon, 1924

MAY 2

On the evening of 2 May 1924, Patrick Mahon, aged thirty-four, went to retrieve a Gladstone bag from the cloakroom at Waterloo Station, London. As he tried to leave the station afterwards he was approached by a police officer, who asked to be shown the bag's contents. Mahon said that he had not got the key, and was then taken to Kennington police station, where keys were found in his possession. Later, at Scotland Yard, the bag was opened and found to contain a cook's knife, a brown canvas bag with the initials E.B.K. and some bloodstained items of clothing.

Unable to account for these articles satisfactorily, Mahon was told that he would be held while inquiries were made. After much hesitation he finally made a statement which led to the discovery of human remains in a bungalow near Eastbourne the following morning. They were the remains of Mahon's mistress, Emily Kaye, who had been dead for over a fortnight and whose body had been dismembered. She had been pregnant at the time of her death.

Mahon, a soda-fountain salesman of Richmond, Surrey,

was a married man with one child. He had a criminal record, having been in trouble on one occasion for forgery, on another for embezzlement and on a third for robbery with violence; the third of these charges had been brought against him in 1916, when he was sent to prison for five years.

A day or two earlier Mahon's wife had found a cloak-room ticket in one of his pockets and asked a friend — a former railway policeman — to find out what had been left at Waterloo Station. The ex-policeman had inspected the bag, looking into it from the side, and reported the matter to the CID. Mrs Mahon had been asked to replace the ticket in her husband's suit.

Emily Kaye, a thirty-eight-year-old shorthand-typist and bookkeeper, was just one of many women with whom Mahon had had affairs. She had been induced to part with most of her savings, thinking that he intended taking her to South Africa — where he would set up home with her — and had joined Mahon in Eastbourne on 12 April, the bungalow having been rented for eight weeks. The exact date of her death was never established.

According to Mahon, who gave several different accounts during the course of the investigation, Emily Kaye had been accidentally killed as a result of a violent quarrel. Having dismembered her body, he had pushed the torso into a trunk — where the police found it — and burnt her head, legs and feet on the sitting-room fire; other parts were cut into small pieces and boiled in a pot or thrown from the window of a train. He had left the bag at Waterloo Station before going back to his home in Richmond.

While some parts of his story were undoubtedly true, others were clearly not — especially as he was found to have bought a cook's knife and a meat-saw in London before going to join the victim in Eastbourne. He was accordingly brought to trial in Lewes in July, with crowds of people mobbing the court-house.

Mahon denied the offence. He said that the victim had demanded that he should leave his wife in order to set up home with her, and that he had rented the bungalow as an 'experiment', in order to show her that this would be unwise. She had been killed, he said, when she hit her head against a coal-scuttle while he was defending himself against her. He was not believed.

On being found guilty, he protested about 'the bitterness and unfairness' of the judge's summing-up. He was, however, hanged at Wandsworth Prison on 9 September 1924.

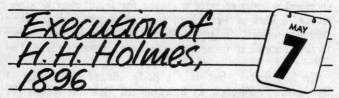

Execution of H.H. Holmes, 1896

MAY 7

H.H. Holmes, who was hanged at Philadelphia's Moyamensing Prison on 7 May 1896, was a mass murderer. His victims included mistresses, employees and acquaintances, but how many of them there were altogether is not known. He was also an insurance swindler and a bigamist.

A native of Gilmanton, New Hampshire, Holmes was born on 16 May 1860; his real name was Hermann Webster Mudgett. He practised medicine in New York for a short while after obtaining a degree at the age of twenty-four, then moved to Chicago, where he worked in a drug-store owned by a Mrs Holden. Later he became the owner of the store, Mrs Holden having mysteriously disappeared.

Holmes had married at eighteen, but deserted his wife and son in 1886, changing his name when he went to Chicago. There he soon married again — it was the first of several such marriages — and he began to swindle one of his new 'wife's' uncles, causing a family quarrel in the process. He also had a succession of mistresses, some of whom disappeared as mysteriously as Mrs Holden.

125

With his business thriving, Holmes bought a vacant lot and began to build a hotel, with turrets, battlements and secret passages, which became known as 'Holmes's Castle'. When this was later investigated by police, it was found that there were air-tight rooms which could be filled with gas from hidden pipes operated from the office, and that the basement contained a kiln large enough to hold a human body.

Holmes sold the drugstore in 1892, after the completion of his hotel. During the following year he had a good many guests to accommodate as a result of the Chicago Exposition. But he was involved in petty crime as well, and received a term of imprisonment for fraud shortly afterwards. It was as a result of a conversation with a fellow prisoner named Hedgspeth in St Louis Prison that he was to find himself in more serious trouble towards the end of 1894.

In September that year a body alleged to be that of Benjamin F. Pitezel, an associate of Holmes' whose life had been insured for $10,000, was found in Philadelphia; he had evidently died as a result of an explosion. Holmes, among others, went to identify the body, and the insurance company paid the $10,000 to Pitezel's wife. On hearing of this, however, Hedgspeth wrote to the company, saying that Holmes had told him about a 'foolproof method' of insurance fraud, and warning them that the body was not that of Pitezel at all.

The company investigated the case and obtained evidence which appeared to substantiate Hedgspeth's allegation. Holmes, on being questioned, agreed that he had defrauded the company using a body which had been provided by a doctor; the real Pitezel, he said, had gone abroad, taking his three children. Mrs Pitezel also admitted fraud, but did not know her husband's whereabouts; she said that Holmes had taken her children to stay with a widow in Kentucky and that she had not seen them since.

Later, however, Holmes confessed that the body in Philadelphia *was* Pitezel's, and said that the dead man had committed suicide; the children were safe in England. But the bodies of two of the children were then found in a cellar in Toronto, and the remains of the third were recovered from a chimney in Irvington.

Holmes was eventually brought to trial on 28 October 1895, for the murder of Benjamin Pitezel, but the case against him included evidence that he had committed other murders, too. The witnesses included a Chicago car mechanic, who told the court that he had been employed by Holmes at the 'castle' to strip the flesh from three corpses which he believed to have been brought from the city mortuary. Holmes, he said, had paid him $36 for each of the bodies so treated.

While under sentence of death Holmes wrote his memoirs for a newspaper, claiming that he had killed twenty-seven people. He afterwards said that the confession was entirely false, and had been written for the sake of sensationalism. On the scaffold he said that he had been responsible for only two deaths and that these were both of women on whom he had performed illegal operations.

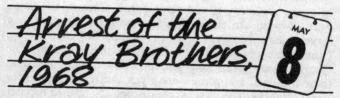

Arrest of the Kray Brothers, 1968

MAY 8

At 6 a.m. on 8 May 1968, teams of detectives raided homes in the East End of London and arrested seventeen members of a criminal gang led by the twin brothers Ronald and Reginald Kray. The gang ran a protection business and was responsible for many acts of brutality, including murder, and the arrests followed a long investigation which had been greatly hampered by the fear of witnesses to give information about them. But once the downfall of the gang seemed certain, these witnesses began to come forward of their own accord, and some of its members agreed to give evidence in return for their own freedom. It thus became possible to bring various charges against the gang leaders and nine other people.

These were all brought to trial together at the Old Bailey in January 1969, the most serious charges concerning the murder of George Cornell, a member of the rival Richardson Gang from south London, the murder of Jack McVitie, a small-time crook known as 'Jack the Hat', and the alleged murder of Frank Mitchell, a well-known escaped convict popularly called 'the Mad Axeman'. Among the witnesses called by the prosecution were the barmaid of a public house in which Cornell had been shot dead in March 1966, and Ronald Hart, a cousin of the Krays, who had been present when McVitie was stabbed to death in a basement flat in Stoke Newington in October 1967.

The trial lasted thirty-nine days, with many sensational disclosures being made, and ten of the prisoners were convicted. Ronald Kray and a henchman named John Barrie were both sentenced to life imprisonment for Cornell's murder, Reggie Kray being given ten years for being an accessory to the same crime. Both of the twins were given life sentences, with a recommendation that they serve at least thirty years, for the murder of Jack McVitie. Other members of the gang, including their older brother Charles, were given long sentences for crimes related to these murders, and some were given shorter sentences for lesser offences. The charges concerning the alleged murder of Frank Mitchell, whose body was never found, were not proved.

The Kray twins, aged thirty-five, were both former professional boxers. Outwardly they were respectable businessmen, owning clubs and restaurants, and had many celebrities among their friends. But, in fact, they enjoyed their reputation for violence and the power which it gave them. 'I saw beatings that were unnecessary even by underworld standards and witnessed people slashed with a razor just for the hell of it,' said Ronald Hart, who had worked for them. On one occasion, after shooting somebody, Reggie Kray had said to him, 'You want to try it some time. It's a nice feeling.'

'We were well aware that many people thought we had bitten off more than we could chew in arresting a large number of known criminals without, at that time, having sufficient evidence to secure conviction,' Commander John du Rose later recorded. 'But we were convinced that once the Gang was in custody evidence would be forthcoming. Events proved us right but there was still a lot of work to be done verifying statements and digging up fresh facts. Nothing was left to chance and a vast team of detectives worked day and night.'

While serving an earlier sentence for grievous bodily harm Ronald Kray, a homosexual, was certified insane and transferred to a mental hospital in Surrey. In 1979 he was again found to be insane, and this time he was committed to Broadmoor.

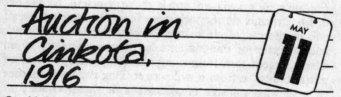

Auction in Cinkota, 1916

MAY 11

On 11 May 1916, a house with an adjoining workshop in the village of Cinkota, near Budapest, was sold by public auction. The owner was not present and his whereabouts were unknown; the sale had been ordered by the district court so that unpaid taxes on the property could be collected. It was bought by Istvan Molnar, a middle-aged blacksmith, who intended turning it into a smithy and general repair shop.

A week or so after Molnar and his family had moved into the house seven large tin barrels were discovered behind sheets of corrugated iron in the workshop; they were sealed and unexpectedly heavy. At first Molnar paid no attention to them, but when they were eventually opened each was found to contain the body of a naked woman.

The women, whose ages varied between thirty and fifty, had all been strangled, their deaths taking place over a period of two or three years; there was no means by which any of the bodies could be identified. Moreover, the property had previously been occupied by an unknown tenant who had rarely been seen by neighbours and who had left no personal belongings or papers which would have enabled the police to trace him.

After the investigation had dragged on for about three weeks without progress, Geza Bialokurszky, one of Budapest's most experienced detectives, was put in charge of it. Searching lists of missing persons, he came across an entry concerning a thirty-six-year-old spinster named Anna Novak who had disappeared five years earlier while employed as a cook by the widow of a Hussar colonel.

Bialokurszky questioned the widow and learnt that the missing cook's trunk was still in the attic where she had left it. Fingerprints on the lock were found to match those of one of the corpses from the Cinkota 'House of Horror', and a search of the contents led to the discovery of an advertisement torn from a popular daily newspaper. This purported to be from a widower seeking the acquaintance of a mature spinster or widow, with the possibility of marriage in mind. A post office box number was given for replies.

Bialokurszky made inquiries at the central post office in Budapest and found that the box-holder had given his name as Elemer Nagy; the address he gave was that of an empty plot of land in one of the suburbs. A search of back numbers of the newspaper revealed that the same box number had been used in over twenty advertisements of

130

the same type during a period of less than two years. One of these had been paid for with a postal order, the advertiser using the same name but giving a false address in Cinkota. The others had been paid for in cash.

A facsimile of the signature on the postal order was published in the newspapers, and two days later a domestic servant named Rosa Diosi informed Bialokurszky that it was the handwriting of her former lover, Bela Kiss, who had been called up on the outbreak of war. She produced a postcard which he had sent her from a prisoner-of-war camp in October 1914, asking her to forward some underwear which had been left in her care; the handwriting had the same characteristics as the postal order signature, and Bialokurszky was certain that Bela Kiss was the 'Monster of Cinkota'.

Other women who had known him as a result of his advertisements came forward to provide further information, and finally a photograph was obtained. From this he was recognized as a frequent visitor to Budapest's red-light district.

Towards the end of the year five more bodies, all of naked women, were found under flowerbeds in Istvan Molnar's garden.

By this time it was known that, prior to committing his first murder Bela Kiss, a plumber by trade, had been in the practice of seducing middle-aged women, mainly servants, and coaxing them into parting with their savings. He had used the money to pay for the services of prostitutes, for which he appeared to have an almost insatiable need. He had started killing his victims after one of them had become too demanding for him.

Bela Kiss was never brought to justice, and what became of him is not known. Bialokurszky, who tried for years to trace him, became convinced that he had died in captivity after being wounded in battle. But his disappearance inevitably gave rise to a variety of legends, and some people claimed to have seen him in America long after the war ended.

131

Trial of Peter Manuel, 1958

On 12th May 1958, thirty-one-year-old Peter Manuel was brought to trial in Glasgow, charged with eight murders. The case lasted fourteen days, during the course of which the defendant dismissed his counsel and took over the defence himself. The evidence for the prosecution included Manuel's own confession, but he claimed that this had been made as a result of police threats to charge other members of his family in connection with the offences. The defendant was found guilty on all but one of the charges and sentenced to death. While awaiting execution he confessed to three other murders.

Manuel, a habitual criminal with a record of theft and rape, had been arrested following the discovery of a triple murder in Uddingston, south of Glasgow, at the beginning of the year. Peter Smart, a self-made businessman, his wife and their eleven-year-old son had been shot dead during a burglary at their home on 1 January, their bodies being found some days afterwards. Manuel, who lived with his parents, was suspected and housebreaking tools were found at his home. He and his father were both detained.

While in custody Manuel said that he would give the information which the police wanted on condition that his father was released. Later he admitted being responsible for the triple murder, and also said that he had killed seventeen-year-old Anne Kneilands in East Kilbride two years earlier, three members of a family living just outside East Kilbride in September 1956, and another seventeen-year-old girl, Isabelle Cooke, near her home in Mount Vernon a few days before the murder of Peter Smart and his family.

In the first triple murder case, as in the second, the

132

victims had all been shot during the course of a burglary. The two seventeen-year-old girls had both been the victims of sex murders, Anne Kneilands being found on a golf course with some items of clothing missing. Isabelle Cooke in a shallow grave, almost naked. It was in the case of Anne Kneilands that Manuel was acquitted for lack of evidence. In the case of Isabelle Cooke it was the murderer himself who showed police where the victim had been buried.

'This is the place,' he said. 'In fact, I think I'm standing on her now.'

Born in 1927, Manuel had been almost constantly in trouble from 1939 onwards. His first conviction was for burglary, for which he was put on probation. Soon afterwards he was sent to an approved school, from which he escaped eleven times, for housebreaking. He was then sent to Borstal for robbery and indecent assault — his first known sexual offence. Then, in 1946, he was jailed for housebreaking and rape, and served seven years before being released in 1953. He was again in prison between October 1956 and November 1957.

The three murders to which he confessed while under sentence of death were those of Helen Carlin, a prostitute found strangled in Pimlico in September 1954, Anne Steele, a fifty-five-year-old spinster who was battered to death in Glasgow in January 1956, and Ellen Petrie, who was stabbed, also in Glasgow, in June 1956.

On 8 December 1957, Sydney Dunn, a Newcastle taxi-driver, was found dead on the moors at Edmondbyers, County Durham; he had been shot in the head and his throat had been cut. A coroner's inquest found that he, too, had been killed by Peter Manuel.

Following the dismissal of his appeal, Manuel was hanged at Glasgow's Barlinnie Prison on 11 July 1958.

Discovery of ancient skull, 1983

On 13 May 1983, workers digging in a Cheshire peat bog found a woman's skull which, though over 1500 years old, was so well preserved that it still contained parts of the brain, hair and ligaments. Because of its good condition, nobody at the time suspected its age, and a pathologist who examined it said that it was part of the body of a woman who had allegedly been murdered in the same area in 1960 or 1961. This mistake led to the conviction of Peter Reyn-Bardt, a fifty-seven-year-old former airline official, a few months later.

Reyn-Bardt, a homosexual, had married Malika Maria de Fernandez, a thirty-two-year-old part-time waitress, on 28 March 1959. At the time he was a BOAC executive at Manchester Ringway airport, fearing that discovery of his homosexuality would lead to prosecution and the loss of his job. He saw marriage as a means of acquiring an appearance of respectability. But when his wife realized this her attitude towards him changed, and she started to leave him for months at a time.

Reyn-Bardt set up home on his own in a cottage in Wilmslow, a suburb of Manchester, where his wife suddenly appeared some months later. After a bitter quarrel over money he strangled her, then hacked her body to pieces with an axe and buried the remains in his large wooded garden. In 1963 he moved to Portsmouth.

Twelve years later, still in Portsmouth, he met Paul Russell Corrigan, with whom he was arrested and sent to prison for abducting boys for sexual purposes. When Corrigan, following his release in January 1981, fell foul of the law again — this time he had tortured and killed a boy in Birmingham — he told the police how Reyn-Bardt had murdered his wife.

Now living in Knightsbridge, London, Reyn-Bardt was questioned about his wife's disappearance but denied having killed her. However, the discovery of the ancient skull 300 yards from the cottage in Wilmslow led to further questioning, and Reyn-Bardt, confronted with the 'evidence', then made a confession. In December 1983, after a three-day trial at Chester Crown Court, he was sentenced to life imprisonment.

By this time tests carried out at the radio-carbon dating laboratory at Oxford University had shown the skull from the peat bog to be that of a woman who had died, aged between thirty and fifty, about AD 410.

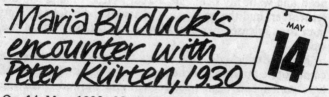

Maria Budlick's encounter with Peter Kürten, 1930

On 14 May 1930, Maria Budlick, a twenty-one-year-old domestic servant, left her home in Cologne to look for work in Düsseldorf, twenty miles away. Arriving at Düsseldorf station, she met a man who offered to show her the way to a hostel, and set off through the streets in his company. But when he tried to persuade her to go into the Volksgarten Park with him she refused.

At this time the city was being terrorized by the 'Monster of Düsseldorf', a brutal sadist responsible for many shocking crimes, and Maria Budlick was unwilling to go into the park with a stranger who, for all she knew, may have been 'the Monster' himself. However, her refusal led to an argument which continued until a second man intervened, asking 'Is everything all right?' The first man then took himself off.

The servant girl's rescuer was a soft-spoken, courteous man — the sort she could trust. Grateful for his help, she went with him to his one-room flat in Mettmännerstrasse, where he gave her a glass of milk and a sandwich. Afterwards they went by tram together to the edge of the city, Maria believing that she was being taken to a hostel, then got out to walk in the Grafenburg Woods. Suddenly the man stopped.

'Do you know now where you are?' he asked. 'I can tell you. You are alone with me in the middle of the woods. Now you scream as much as you like and nobody will hear you!'

At this, he seized her by the throat and tried to rape her. The terrified girl put up a struggle, but had almost lost consciousness when the man unexpectedly loosened his grip. 'Do you remember where I live, in case you're ever in need and want my help?' he asked. Maria, though she *did* remember, had the good sense to say that she did not. The man then released her and showed her the way out of the woods.

Maria Budlick did not report the attack, but when it came to the attention of the police (as a result of a letter of hers which had been misdirected) she showed them the building where she had been taken by her attacker. While they were there the man appeared; he entered his room after seeing the servant girl outside, then left a few minutes later. He was found to be Peter Kürten, a forty-seven-year-old married man with convictions for theft and assault, who had spent a total of over twenty years in prison. He was a factory worker and a keen trade unionist.

Though not questioned at the time, Kürten was arrested a week later after his wife had informed the police that he had confessed to being the 'Monster of Düsseldorf'. He admitted sixty-eight crimes, including the nine murders and seven attempted murders for which he was brought to trial in April the following year. It seems that after seeing Maria Budlick at the building in Mettmännerstrasse he had told his wife about his crimes so that she could claim a reward for his capture, knowing that he would soon be arrested anyway.

Kürten, described at his trial as 'the king of sexual delinquents', was stimulated to the point of orgasm by the sight of blood or fire. Unlike most other known sadists, he killed both men and women — and also children and animals. Moreover, to the spectators in the Düsseldorf courtroom it was evident that he derived pleasure from describing his crimes in detail.

Though a defence of insanity was made on his behalf, he was found guilty on all counts, and sentence of death was pronounced nine times. He was calm and courteous to the end, and before being executed by guillotine on 2 July 1931, said that it would give him much pleasure to hear the sound of his own blood gushing from his neck after the sentence had been carried out.

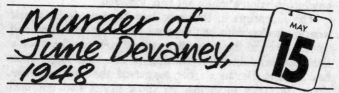

Murder of June Devaney, 1948

MAY 15

During the early hours of 15 May 1948, June Anne Devaney, aged three years and eleven months, was found to be missing from a ground-floor children's ward of the Queen's Park Hospital in Blackburn, Lancashire. The discovery was made by Staff Nurse Gwendoline Humphreys, who found the child's cot empty when she entered the ward just before 1 a.m. It appeared from a trail of footprints on the polished floor that she had been removed by an intruder.

Nurse Humphreys raised the alarm and a search of the hospital and its grounds was started. Just under two and a half hours later the missing child was found dead about

100 yards from the ward. She had been raped and then brutally murdered, her assailant holding her by the leg and dashing her head against one of the boundary walls.

The crime was such an atrocious one that the Chief Constable of Blackburn feared an outbreak of public disorder. He called on Scotland Yard for assistance without delay, hoping to bring the culprit to justice quickly, and within a few hours Detective Chief Inspector John Capstick and Detective Sergeant John Stoneman arrived to take charge of the investigation. But it was to take them three months to find the person responsible.

June Devaney, the daughter of a miner, had been admitted to hospital on 5 May suffering from mild pneumonia, but had made a good recovery and was due to be discharged on the morning of her murder. Though under four years of age, she was the oldest child in the ward and the only one who could talk. It would therefore not have been possible for any of the other five children, even if they had been awake at the time, to give the police any information about what had occurred.

The footprints in the ward had been made by a man wearing socks, who had entered by the door at one end, walked over to the cots, then moved towards the door at the other end before returning to the first door; those beside June Devaney's cot suggested that he had stood there for some moments. As these prints had not been made by any member of the hospital staff, it was assumed that they had been made by the murderer.

It seemed, too, that the person concerned had taken a Winchester bottle containing sterile water from a nearby trolley and placed it under June's cot, for Nurse Humphreys remembered that it had been in its usual place when she went into the ward prior to the child's disappearance. An examination of this bottle by a finger-print expert resulted in the discovery of several fresh prints which had also not been left by any of the staff. But when photographs of these were sent to Scotland Yard they were found not to match those of any known criminal.

Capstick believed that the murderer was a local man with a knowledge of the hospital; he therefore proposed that every male person in Blackburn between the ages of fourteen and ninety who was not bedridden should be fingerprinted. The Mayor of Blackburn made a public announcement about this, calling for co-operation from the town's 110,000 inhabitants and promising that all the fingerprints would be destroyed after they had been compared with those of June Devaney's murderer. He then set an example by becoming Capstick's first volunteer.

It was a tremendous undertaking, but Capstick was certain that it would eventually lead to the solution of the crime. Suddenly, on the afternoon of 12 August after 46,000 sets of prints had been checked, one of the experts scrutinizing the latest batch exclaimed, 'I've got him! It's here!'

That evening Peter Griffiths, a twenty-two-year-old former Guardsman working as a flour-mill packer, was arrested as he left his home in Birley Street, in one of the town's poorest districts. On being charged and cautioned, he admitted the offence, saying that he had had a number of drinks beforehand. He had abducted the child from the ward after removing his shoes, and had later beaten her head against the wall to stop her crying, he said.

The suit which he had worn on the night in question was examined and found to have been stained with June Devaney's blood; fibres taken from it were identical to others found on the dead girl's body. Though police suspected that Griffiths had also murdered an eleven-year-old boy in Farnworth earlier the same year, they were not able to obtain a second confession.

At his trial at the Lancashire Assizes, it was suggested that Griffiths, a solitary person who drank heavily, was suffering from a form of mental illness and was not responsible for his actions. But the jury took only twenty-three minutes to find him guilty and he was sentenced to death. He was hanged at Walton Prison on 19 November 1948.

Disappearance of Camille Holland, 1899

During the early evening of 19 May 1899, Miss Camille Holland, aged fifty-six, left her farmhouse near Saffron Walden in the company of her lover, fifty-three-year-old Samuel Dougal, telling their maid that she was going shopping and would not be long. Two hours later Dougal returned alone, saying that she had gone to London and would be back shortly. However, she did not return at all that day, and the following morning Dougal informed the maid that he had received a letter from Miss Holland, saying that she was going on a holiday. In fact, she was dead, but four years were to elapse before her body was discovered.

Miss Holland, a wealthy woman, had been living with Dougal as his wife for several months. She had bought the farm, which Dougal renamed Moat House Farm, in January, and they had moved into it on 27 April after staying in lodgings in Saffron Walden in the meantime. The day after her disappearance a younger woman moved in to take her place, bringing a little girl. Though Dougal began introducing this newcomer as his widowed daughter, it later turned out that she was his legal wife.

Dougal, an ex-soldier with a prison record for forgery, had been married three times; his first two wives had died in Nova Scotia, where he had served for ten years, and his third marriage had taken place in Dublin in 1892. He had had four children by his first wife and two by his third, in addition to an unknown number by other women. His third marriage ended in divorce in 1902 after Mrs Dougal had run away with an engine-driver. Dougal himself, whatever his marital state, was rarely without a mistress for long, and sometimes had several at the same time.

Soon after Miss Holland's disappearance he began to transfer money from her bank account to his own by means of forgery; he managed to become the owner of Moat House Farm in the same way. He was thus able to buy himself a car and spend much of his time hunting, shooting and drinking, as well as having affairs, without any financial difficulties. But Miss Holland's continued absence gave rise to rumours, and eventually one of the forgeries was discovered. A police investigation then became inevitable.

In March 1903 Dougal fled. He was arrested in London, with £563 in banknotes and gold and many valuables in his possession, and charged with forging a cheque. The following day he was taken to the police station in Saffron Walden, and a search of Moat House Farm was started.

Five weeks later Miss Holland's body was recovered from an old drainage ditch. She had been shot in the back of the head at close range, the bullet having been fired from a revolver owned by Dougal. The ex-soldier was charged with her murder on 30 April.

He was brought to trial in Chelmsford on 22 June. The following day, having given no evidence, he was convicted and sentenced to death. After an appeal had been dismissed, he wrote a long letter to the Home Secretary, claiming that he had shot Miss Holland by accident, but this was to no avail and he was hanged at Chelmsford Prison on 8 July 1903.

He admitted his guilt on the scaffold.

Murder of Bobby Franks, 1924

On 21 May 1924, Bobby Franks, fourteen-year-old son of a millionaire businessman, was abducted outside his school in the Chicago suburb of South Side Kenwood. The boy's mother received a telephone call, informing her that he had been kidnapped and that a ransom note would be sent through the post. The caller gave his name as Mr Johnson.

The following day a demand for $10,000 was received, the note stating that the missing boy was 'at present well and safe'. But before anything could be done about it the police informed Bobby Franks' father that a boy's body had been found in a culvert by the Pennsylvania railroad tracks.

In spite of facial disfiguration caused by hydrochloric acid, the body was quickly identified as Bobby Franks. His skull was fractured and he had been strangled.

A week later a pair of spectacles which had been found near the body were traced to Nathan Leopold Jr, a nineteen-year-old law student at Chicago University. Leopold, an amateur ornithologist, agreed that the spectacles were his and said that he must have dropped them in the culvert while bird-watching in the area some time previous to the murder. However, there were no weather marks on them, and this suggested that he was lying, as there had been a lot of rain prior to the date of the murder. Leopold was therefore regarded as a suspect.

Asked what he had been doing on the afternoon of 21 May, he said that he and his friend Richard Loeb, an eighteen-year-old fellow student, had been out with two girls, whose names were Mae and Edna. But, while Loeb corroborated this, neither he nor Leopold could give any information which enabled the police to trace these girls.

Moreover, specimens of Leopold's typing were found to match that of the ransom note. Leopold and Loeb who both, like Bobby Franks, had extremely wealthy parents and were accordingly questioned at length. Loeb eventually confessed; then Leopold confessed, too. They were brought to trial for murder and kidnapping in July the same year.

Besides being accustomed to wealth and luxury, the two defendants were both intellectually gifted, Leopold having an I.Q. of 200. But they were bored and had decided to commit a 'perfect' murder after failing to derive sufficient excitement from a series of petty thefts. Bobby Franks, a friend of Loeb's younger brother, had not been chosen as their victim because they disliked him; he had merely been an easy person to entice into a hired car. The crime, in the words of their lawyer, Clarence Darrow, had been a 'senseless, useless, purposeless, motiveless act of two boys'.

A plea that both defendants were mentally ill — Leopold being a paranoiac and Loeb a schizophrenic — probably saved their lives, for at the end of the trial each was sentenced to life imprisonment for murder and ninety-nine years for kidnapping. The failure of the judge to impose the death penalty, however, caused grave public disquiet and continued to be a contentious matter for years afterwards.

The case was brought back into the headlines in January 1936, when Richard Loeb was murdered by a fellow convict.

Nathan Leopold served thirty-three years, during which he ran educational rehabilitation courses for other prisoners and volunteered to take part in anti-malaria experiments. Following his release in 1958, he went to Puerto Rico, where he married in 1961. He died ten years later.

Questioning of Wayne Williams, 1981

MAY 22

During the early hours of 22 May 1981, a police surveillance team on patrol near the Chattahoochee River in Atlanta, Georgia, heard the sound of a splash and saw a young black man driving away from the scene in a station-wagon. They stopped the man for questioning but afterwards let him go, as they appeared to have no cause to arrest him. However, they remained suspicious, and the man — Wayne Williams, a twenty-three-year-old music-talent promoter and freelance photographer — was placed under observation. Two days later, when the body of Nathaniel Cater, aged twenty-seven, was found floating in the river, Williams was suspected of murder.

Cater had been seen leaving a theatre with Williams just before his disappearance, the witness informing police that the two men had been holding hands. It was found, too, that dog hairs on Cater's body were similar to others found at Williams' home and inside his station-wagon. But by this time Williams was suspected not only of Cater's murder but also of twenty-seven others.

The twenty-seven other people who had been murdered were all young blacks, teenagers and children of both sexes whose bodies had been found in Atlanta during the previous two years. The crimes had been committed without apparent motive — except in the case of a girl who had been raped — and by a variety of means, including suffocation, strangulation, shooting and stabbing. They were believed by blacks to be the work of a white racist, and the police had been subjected to much criticism over their failure to catch him.

Their inquiries now established that Williams had been seen in the company of two of these other victims, and laboratory tests on fibres, as well as dog hairs, from his home showed that he had been connected with another eight. Though he was charged only with the murder of Nathaniel Cater and one other person — Jimmy Payne, the twenty-sixth victim — his arrest brought this long series of crimes to an end.

Wayne Williams, an intelligent and resourceful man, was a homosexual with a hatred of other blacks and a frustrated desire for instant personal success. The evidence against him was entirely circumstantial but at his trial, which began in January 1982, the prosecution was allowed to produce evidence relating to other murders besides those with which he was charged. This, together with the sudden cessation of the murders, weighed heavily against him, and he was convicted on both counts.

He was sentenced to two consecutive terms of life imprisonment.

Execution of Frederick Deeming, 1892

MAY 23

On 23 May 1892, Frederick Deeming, a multiple murderer and confidence trickster aged about fifty, was hanged in Melbourne, Australia. A large number of officials and newspaper reporters were present, and the hangman and his assistant both wore false beards to prevent themselves being identified. A crowd of 10,000 people waited outside the prison while the execution was carried out.

Deeming, the youngest of seven children, had been born in Liverpool. A flamboyant and charming man, he travelled a great deal, committing many thefts and frauds with ease; women were generally fascinated by him. He married an English girl who bore him four children, but abandoned her twice — once in Australia and once in South Africa. It was because she pursued him that she was finally murdered.

In 1891 Deeming took up residence in Rainhill, to the east of Liverpool, claiming to be Mr Albert Williams, an Inspector of Regiments. He let it be known that he was looking for a house on behalf of Baron Brook, a personal friend, and went to look over a nearby villa which the owner, Mrs Mather, wanted to let furnished to a suitable tenant. Having reached an agreement with Mrs Mather, he was allowed to move into the property without paying any rent in advance, in order to prepare for the Baron's arrival. He then began to court Mrs Mather's daughter Emily, aged twenty-five, who believed him to be a bachelor.

Before long, however, Deeming's wife arrived unexpectedly, bringing their four children, and insisted on moving into the villa with him. When Emily Mather heard about this, Deeming told her that Mrs Deeming was his sister, and that she had brought her children to spend a short holiday with him before going to join her husband abroad. Emily Mather was evidently satisfied with this explanation.

Deeming asked Mrs Mather's permission to cement the ground under the floor of the villa so that the floorboards would lie more evenly and provide surfaces suitable for some valuable carpets owned by Baron Brook. Mrs Mather agreed to this, and Deeming started the work himself. By the time he had finished his wife and four children had been murdered and their bodies buried in the cement. He employed a local carpenter to re-lay the floorboards.

A short while after this Deeming told Mrs Mather that he had to go to Australia and that Baron Brook would not be moving into the villa after all. He then married Emily, and they set sail together, arriving in Melbourne in December 1891.

'Mrs Williams', however, was soon to be disposed of in the same way as Mrs Deeming and her children: about 20 December her body was buried in cement under the dining-

146

room hearth of a small furnished house which the couple had rented in Andrew Street, Windsor. She had been struck on the head six times and her throat had been cut. But this time Deeming was more careless and the body was discovered by the owner of the house.

Deeming was arrested in Perth in March 1892, just in time to prevent him marrying an heiress named Kate Rounsevell. By the time he appeared for trial, charged with the murder of Emily Mather, the remains of his wife and children had been discovered and he had been accused in newspaper articles of both crimes, as well as many others.

He pleaded that he was insane, then, towards the end of the trial, made a long speech denying the allegations which had been made against him and describing the spectators in the courtroom as 'the ugliest race of people I have ever seen'.

He died unrepentant, smoking a cigar as he walked to the place of execution.

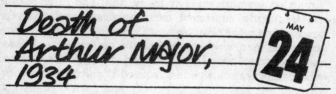

Death of Arthur Major, 1934

MAY
24

On 24 May 1934, Arthur Major, a forty-four-year-old lorry-driver of Kirkby-on-Bain, Lincolnshire, died in agony after a short illness. His wife Ethel, who was two years younger, told their doctor that her husband had died during the night after having 'another of his fits'. The doctor therefore put Major's death down to 'status epilepticus', and arrangements were made for the funeral. But the following day the local police received a remarkable anonymous letter, signed 'Fairplay'. It read:

'Have you ever heard of a wife poisoning her husband?

147

Look further into the death of Mr Major of Kirkby-on-Bain. Why did he complain of his food tasting nasty and throw it away to a neighbour's dog, which has since died? Ask the undertaker if he looked natural after death. Why did he stiffen so quickly? Why was he so jerky when dying? I myself have heard her threaten to poison him years ago. In the name of the law, I beg you to analyse the contents of his stomach.'

The police discovered that Arthur Major had been a drunken bully, whose fourteen-year-old son regularly slept at his grandfather's house, a mile away, to avoid him. Ethel Major, after being questioned, suddenly turned to the police officer concerned and asked: 'I'm not under suspicion, am I? I haven't done anything wrong!' The police officer gave a non-committal answer, then went to see the neighbour whose dog had died; the body was dug up so that its stomach contents could be examined. The next day Arthur Major's funeral was called off by order of the coroner, so that the contents of *his* stomach could be examined, too. Both the dog and the lorry-driver were found to have died from strychnine poisoning.

Further inquiries revealed that Arthur and Ethel Major had frequently quarrelled over the dead man's alleged affair with a neighbour's wife and his own wife's expenditure on clothes which he considered unnecessary. It was also discovered that Ethel's father, Tom Brown, was a retired gamekeeper, who had frequently killed vermin with poison.

When Ethel Major was asked if she knew about this, she replied, 'I didn't know where he kept his poisons. I never at any time had any poison in the house.' She then revealed that she knew more about the cause of her husband's death than had so far been made known to anyone except the police, for she added, 'I didn't know that my husband died of strychnine.'

Tom Brown showed the police a locked box which he kept in his bedroom; it contained a bottle of strychnine crystals. He informed them that his daughter knew the contents, but would not have been able to use them as the key to the box had been lost more than ten years previously and had not been replaced. The key was later found in Ethel Major's possession.

Ethel Major was brought to trial for her husband's murder at the Lincoln Assizes in November 1934, convicted and sentenced to death. Despite a strong recommendation of mercy from the jury, she was hanged at Hull Prison on 19 December the same year.

Death of 'Pigsticker' Ayres, 1931

MAY 30

On the night of 30 May 1931, Herbert Ayres, a forty-five-year-old casual labourer known as 'Pigsticker', was attacked and killed in an area of woodland and makeshift huts near Elstree, in Hertfordshire. The crime was committed by two other labourers and witnessed by a third, but nothing was reported until three days later, when the victim's charred body was found in a smouldering refuse tip at Scratchwood Sidings, half a mile away. It was then found that he had died as a result of a heavy blow on the head which had fractured his skull.

There were a large number of navvies in the area, all living in shacks and known to each other by nicknames. When the police began making inquiries, the one who had witnessed the crime — a fellow named Armstrong — told them what had happened, identifying the culprits as 'Moosh' and 'Tiggy', two men who shared a hut and kept three dogs to protect it. According to his account, Armstrong had been staying the night in this hut, and had been dozing on the floor when he heard a quarrel going on

149

outside. He had then looked out and seen 'Moosh' and 'Tiggy' beating up 'Pigsticker'. Afterwards, he said, they took the body away in a sack, carrying it over a pole.

'Moosh' and 'Tiggy' were found to be William Shelley, aged fifty-seven, and Oliver Newman, sixty-one, both of whom had the reputation of being tough and disagreeable. To the police officers who went to arrest them, their dogs seemed tough and disagreeable as well, and the officers concerned waited outside the shack for some hours until its occupants gave themselves up. The arrests were followed by the discovery of a bloodstained axe under the floor of the hut.

Shelley and Newman admitted having caused Ayres' death, but claimed that they had only used their fists. They said that the dead man had been in the habit of stealing from them, and that on the night in question they had found some bacon and bread to be missing from their hut. They had therefore beaten him up and, on realizing that they had killed him, buried his body in the tip.

The two men were brought to trial at the Old Bailey, the case lasting two days. Both were convicted and sentenced to death, Shelley afterwards commenting that the sentence was twenty years late. They were hanged on 5 August 1931.

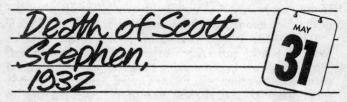

Death of Scott Stephen, 1932

MAY 31

During the early hours of 31 May 1932, Elvira Barney, a wealthy twenty-seven-year-old socialite, telephoned her doctor in a hysterical state and told him that there had been 'a terrible accident' at her home in Knightsbridge,

London. The doctor hurried to her address, 21, William's Mews, and found Michael Scott Stephen, her twenty-four-year-old lover, lying dead on the stairs. He had been shot in the chest at close range.

The police were called, and a Smith and Wesson revolver with two empty chambers was found near the body. Mrs Barney, who was separated from her husband, had been out to a party with Stephen earlier and, on returning, they had started to quarrel over another woman. According to her own statement, Mrs Barney had then threatened to commit suicide, using the gun which she kept at her bedside, and Stephen had been accidentally killed when he tried to take it away from her.

But neighbours who had been woken up by the quarrel told the police that Mrs Barney had actually threatened to shoot *him*, and that the threat had been followed by the shot or shots. On 3 June Mrs Barney was arrested and charged with murder.

At her trial at the Old Bailey the following month witnesses gave evidence that the accused and her lover had often quarrelled, and one — a chauffeur's wife — claimed that on an earlier occasion Mrs Barney had leant out of the window and fired at him while he was in the mews below.

The firearms expert, Robert Churchill, stated that the gun which had been used was one of the safest types in existence and that considerable pressure was needed to fire it. This evidence, however, was challenged by the defence counsel, Sir Patrick Hastings, who pointed out that there was no safety catch and proceeded to press the trigger several times without apparent difficulty. 'It doesn't seem to require any terrific muscular strength,' he remarked as he did so.

Mrs Barney stuck to her story that Stephen had been killed by accident. Her counsel, after asking for the gun to be placed on the edge of the witness-box, suddenly ordered her to pick it up. The fact that she automatically picked it up with her right hand served to cast doubt on the evidence of the chauffeur's wife, who had said that Mrs Barney had

151

fired with her left hand on the earlier occasion.

The jury deliberated for an hour and fifty minutes before returning a verdict of not guilty. Mrs Barney then left the court and found herself applauded by a large crowd outside.

Four years later she was found dead in a hotel in Paris.

Mrs. Freeman Lee found murdered, 1948

On 1 June 1948, a milkman on his delivery round in Maidenhead, Berkshire, called at the home of Mrs Freeman Lee, a ninety-four-year-old recluse, and found two full bottles still standing on the doorstep from previous days. He told a neighbour, who looked through the window of the downstairs room to which Mrs Lee normally confined herself night and day. As she was not there, the neighbour then peered through the letter-box.

He saw cushions lying on the floor of the hall and, beyond them, a black trunk with a woman's shoe beside it. As his eyes became accustomed to the light, he also saw a bunch of keys lying on the floor. He decided to inform the police.

A constable arrived soon afterwards, accompanied by a local solicitor who was a friend of the old lady. Unable to summon her to the door, they forced an entry and began to search the house. There were seventeen rooms altogether, and Mrs Lee was not in any of them; a search of the garden revealed that she was not there either. Finally, as the constable telephoned the police station to make a report, it occurred to the solicitor to open the trunk in the hall.

There, under a lot of old clothes, he found the body of

Mrs Lee. She had been battered over the head and also bound and gagged. It was later established that she had died from suffocation.

Mrs Lee had lived in the same house for about forty years, and was well-known in Maidenhead. It was generally believed that she was rich as, indeed, she had been in the distant past, but she had been very poor in recent years, existing on a small allowance from a legal benevolent society. Besides that, she had suffered a stroke which left her partially paralysed on one side. Her house was in a shocking state of disrepair and disorder; every part of it had been neglected.

Though the pathologist was unable to state with certainty when her death had occurred, it was found that the last person to see her alive — other than her murderer — had been an electrician who called at the house to install an electric boiling-ring during the early evening of 29 May. Clearly, she had been killed sometime between then and the following morning.

Two parts of a single fingerprint, discovered on the lid of a cardboard box, were identified at Scotland Yard; they had been left by George Russell, a housebreaker with a criminal record. When Russell was located in St Albans five days later a scarf which had belonged to the victim was found in his possession.

Russell denied ever having been inside the house, but when confronted with the fingerprint evidence he began to cry and said that he wanted to make a statement. In this, he inadvertently revealed that he knew Mrs Lee's true circumstances. He was therefore arrested and charged with her murder.

George Russell was brought to trial at the Berkshire Assizes, denying the offence. His counsel sought to discredit the prosecution witnesses, but to no avail; he was convicted and sentenced to death. Showing no emotion at this, the prisoner looked round the hushed courtroom, then tweaked his left ear before leaving the dock. His life of crime, which had lasted over twenty years, was brought to an abrupt end when he was hanged at Oxford Prison on 2 December 1948.

Abduction of Grace Budd, 1928

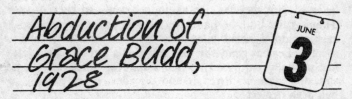

On 3 June 1928, twelve-year-old Grace Budd left her home in New York City in the company of a harmless-looking old man who said that he was taking her to a children's party which was being given by his sister. When she had not returned by 10 p.m. her anxious parents reported the matter to the police. But it was six and a half years before they found out what had become of her — and then they were informed of it in a particularly cruel manner.

The harmless-looking old man, calling himself Frank Howard, had turned up at the home of Edward Budd and his wife on 1 June after seeing an advertisement asking for farm work which their son Paul, aged eighteen, had placed in a newspaper. He said that he owned a large farm in Farmingdale, Long Island, and promised the youth a job there. On the day of the abduction he had lunch with the family at noon, and said that he would take Paul back to Long Island with him when he and Grace returned from the party. The address at which he claimed that the party was being held proved to be non-existent, as did the old man's farm in Long Island.

The police obtained a sample of the man's handwriting from a telegram which he had sent to Paul from Yorkville, Manhattan, on 2 June. They also had an agate container in which he had given the family some cottage cheese; this was found to have been bought from a pedlar in the same vicinity, but provided no distinct fingerprints. There were no other clues to the real identity of 'Frank Howard', and it was not until the morning of 11 November 1934, when Mrs Budd unexpectedly received a letter from him, that any further progress on the case was made.

In this letter, written solely for the purpose of causing further suffering to the missing girl's family, 'Frank Howard' stated that he had murdered Grace and 'feasted on her flesh for nine days'.

'I learned to like the taste of human flesh many years ago during a famine in China,' he said. 'I can't exactly describe the taste. It is something like veal, then again it resembles chicken, only it is tastier than either. The best flesh, that which is most tender, is to be had from children. Little girls have more flavour than little boys.'

The handwriting was identical to the sample which the police had obtained earlier, and the letter had been sent in an envelope which they were able to trace. On 13 December the culprit, whose real name was now known to be Albert Fish, was arrested in a shabby New York City boarding-house. He immediately made a confession, stating that he had originally intended to kill and eat Paul but had changed his mind after seeing Grace. Some hours later he led police to a patch of woodland in Westchester County, where the missing girl's remains had been buried.

The police dug into the frozen earth, working far into the night. Before daylight Grace Budd's skull and bones, together with her clothes, had been recovered.

Albert Fish, then aged sixty-four, was a house painter by trade and the father of six children. He had been arrested many times, and had been sent to prison for writing obscene letters, among other things. But while in custody he admitted to being responsible for numerous other crimes, and is now thought to have criminally assaulted over 100 girls and murdered at least fifteen of them.

He derived sexual pleasure from receiving pain as well as from inflicting it, and an X-ray photograph showed the presence of a large number of needles which he had inserted into his own body.

'There was no known perversion that he did not practise, and practise frequently,' a prison psychiatrist recorded.

Fish was brought to trial for the murder of Grace Budd in White Plains, New York, on 12 March 1935, the judge refusing to allow female spectators into the courtroom in view of the nature of the case. A plea of insanity was made on his behalf, but he was convicted and sentenced to death on 22 March.

'I thought he was insane, but I figured he should be electrocuted anyway,' one of the jurors said later.

Unperturbed by the prospect of his own death, Albert Fish was executed at Sing Sing Prison on 16 January 1936.

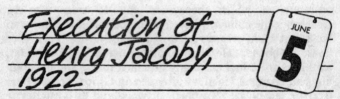

Execution of Henry Jacoby, 1922

JUNE 5

On 5 June 1922, Henry Jacoby, an eighteen-year-old pantry boy, was hanged at Pentonville Prison for the murder of Lady White, sixty-five-year-old widow of a former chairman of the London County Council. Though the crime had been a brutal one, the jury at his trial had made a recommendation of mercy on account of the prisoner's youth, and there had been a lot of agitation in favour of the sentence being commuted. When the execution was carried out within a few days of Ronald True being reprieved (See 6 March), the two cases together were seen by many people as proof of the existence of class privilege.

Lady White, on the morning of 14 March previously, had been found dying from head injuries in her bedroom at the Spencer Hotel in Portman Street, London. There were no signs of a struggle or a forced entry; the murder weapon had not been left at the scene, and nothing appeared to have been stolen. Jacoby, who had only been employed at the hotel for three weeks, was questioned by police and gave information about his background which was found to be false. He was searched and found to have two blood-stained handkerchiefs in his pockets. He finally made a confession of his own accord.

Jacoby said that while lying in bed in the early hours he had been aware of being in a hotel full of rich people, and suddenly decided to steal something from one of the rooms. He got up and took a hammer from a tool bag which some workmen had left in the basement — to 'use if necessary' — then started trying the doors. Finding one unlocked, he entered the room and shone a torch around.

When Lady White woke up and screamed he began to panic and struck her several times with the hammer. He later washed the hammer and wiped it dry with the handkerchiefs before returning it to the tool bag.

Jacoby was held on remand in Brixton Prison, where Ronald True greeted him with his customary joviality. 'Here's another for our Murderers' Club!' he said, slapping him on the back. 'We only accept those who kill them outright!'

Brought to trial at the Old Bailey on 28 April 1922, the prisoner pleaded not guilty. He said in his defence that he thought the person in Lady White's bedroom was an intruder and was afterwards frightened when he realized what he had done. The judge advised the jury that if blows were struck with the intention of inflicting grievous bodily harm and the victim died as a result of them, the assailant was guilty of murder.

When appeals for mercy were dismissed, requests were made for Henry Jacoby to be given a Christian burial. But these were similarly unsuccessful, and his body was interred inside the prison where the hanging took place.

Murder of Mrs. Paterson, 1927

On the evening of 9 June 1927, William Paterson, of Riverton Avenue, Winnipeg, arrived home to find his wife missing. She had left no message for him and their two children did not know what had become of her. Some hours later, when she had still not appeared, he finished putting the children to bed and called the police to find out if any accidents had been reported. They were unable to help him.

Then, suddenly discovering that his suitcase had been forced open and some money stolen, Mr Paterson knelt at his bedside to pray. As he did so, he found his wife's body underneath the bed. Emily Paterson had been beaten to death with a hammer and then raped, her death occurring at approximately eleven o'clock in the morning. Some clothes had also been stolen from the house.

The crime led to the arrest, trial and execution of Earle Nelson, 'the Gorilla Murderer', who, at the age of thirty, had been responsible for many sex killings, mainly in the United States.

Nelson, a strange-looking man with a receding forehead and protruding lips, had hitch-hiked into Winnipeg on 8 June, taking a room in a boarding-house in Smith Street, where he told the landlady that he was 'a religious man of high ideals'. The same day he murdered a fourteen-year-old girl living in the same house and hid her body under the bed of an unoccupied room, where it was found four days later.

After the murder of Mrs Paterson he sold the stolen clothes to a second-hand shop, then went to a barber's to have a shave; the barber noticed that he had blood in his hair. He left Winnipeg in a hurry two days later, after his description had been circulated by the police, and was arrested while hitch-hiking between Wakopa and Bannerman. His trial took place in Winnipeg in November 1927.

Nelson was born in America and brought up by an aunt, his mother having died of venereal disease contracted from his father, when he was nine months old. At the age of ten he was knocked down by a streetcar, receiving injuries which were to cause bouts of pain and dizziness for the rest of his life. In 1918 he was committed to an asylum after an assault on a child, but escaped several times and got married in 1919. His aunt and his wife both gave evidence at his trial, the defence being one of insanity.

Nelson's interest in religion was a genuine one; he had read the Bible avidly as a child, both before and after his accident, and is known to have talked about the subject a lot. But he was also an intensely jealous man — so much so that when his wife was in hospital he immediately began to accuse her of having affairs with the doctors. His marriage lasted only six months.

Of his twenty-two known victims, all but two were killed in America, the first in San Francisco in February 1926. Most were boarding-house landladies, some of them in their fifties or sixties; most were strangled and afterwards raped. The 'Gorilla Murderer' kept on the move and used false names in order to avoid capture. He showed no remorse for his crimes except at the place of execution, when he begged for forgiveness.

He was hanged in Winnipeg on 13 January 1928.

Murder in St. Lucia, 1971

During the early morning of 10 June 1971, an estate house in St Lucia, in the West Indies, was found to be on fire. The alarm was raised by neighbours, but by the time the fire was extinguished the building had been destroyed. The bodies of its two occupants, James and Majorie Etherington, who had been in the banana business, were then found among the debris of a ground-floor bedroom. They were buried on the neighbouring island of Barbados after being viewed, though hardly examined, by the Caribbean Government pathologist.

It was assumed that the fire had been started by accident, and the police at first gave it little attention. But a day or two later an insurance company investigator went to the site and found evidence of arson. A louvred window of the rear scullery, which the fire had not reached, had been broken from the outside, and footprints were found on the floor beneath it. A piece of plastic hose, smelling of petrol, led from the house to the garage, where a car was found with its petrol tank open.

When these discoveries were reported the police took the matter more seriously, and asked Scotland Yard to provide assistance. The local police commissioner, learning that a number of men had been seen hanging about near the Etheringtons' home on the evening before the fire, had three known criminals named Florius, Faucher and Charles held for questioning. 'If I get any real trouble on the island, I bring these three in,' he explained to Professor Keith Simpson, the Home Office Pathologist. 'If they haven't done it, they always know who has!'

Florius, the ringleader, had burn marks on his neck and arm, and he and Anthony Charles — 'who just does what he's told' — both had scratches which suggested that they had been involved in a struggle. The three men admitted having robbed the Etheringtons, and said that the couple had been tied up during the course of the crime. But they denied having used violence or starting the fire.

When the bodies were exhumed for a more thorough examination James Etherington's skull was found to have been smashed in with a blunt instrument, though he was still alive when the fire started. His wife had been gagged as well as bound, and she, too, had died in the fire.

Florius, Faucher and Charles were charged with murder, and brought to trial in Castries, the capital of St Lucia, three months later. The result was a foregone conclusion, and during a speech from the dock Faucher told the court that the victims had been burnt to death deliberately, as Florius had believed that electronic records could otherwise be made of their thoughts. All three were found guilty and subsequently hanged.

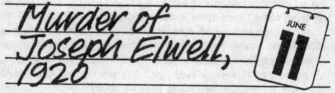

Murder of Joseph Elwell, 1920
JUNE 11

On the morning of 11 June 1920, Joseph Elwell, a well-known bridge expert, was found slumped in a chair in his New York home, with a bullet wound in his forehead. The discovery was made by his housekeeper when she arrived at the house about 8 a.m., at which time Elwell was still alive. He was immediately rushed to hospital, where he died a little while afterwards. The revelations which followed provided much entertainment for the general public, but did not help the New York police in their attempts to solve the crime.

Elwell, aged forty-five, was a rich man and a known philanderer. His two books, *Elwell on Bridge* and *Elwell's Advanced Bridge*, were widely read in the United States, and enabled him to move in high society. He was also thought to be handsome and young-looking, though this impression was due to his wigs and false teeth. At the time of the shooting he was not wearing either, so when his housekeeper arrived she saw him as a bald and toothless man whom she did not recognize. Joseph Elwell had been shot as he sat in his pyjamas, reading letters which had arrived in the morning's post.

Though married in 1904, Elwell had been separated from his wife for some years. Among his possessions police found a list of women's names and addresses, which the newspapers described as a 'love index'. A pile of women's underwear was also found, though the dead man was known to have been living on his own. His companion of the previous evening had been Viola Kraus, who had just been divorced; they had dined together and then been to a show before Elwell returned home in the early hours of the morning. He had afterwards made a number of telephone calls from his bedroom, including one about 6 a.m., when he tried to call a number in Garden City.

As the weapon with which Elwell had been shot was a .45 calibre army revolver, the culprit was thought to be almost certainly a man — and the fact that $400 in cash and items of jewellery had been left untouched suggested that theft had not been the motive. Police officers interviewed all of his known acquaintances, both male and female, and heard various rumours about lovers, husbands and fellow bridge-players, all motivated by jealousy. Yet no real suspect emerged, and nobody has since been able to provide us with one.

The murder of Joseph Elwell remains one of New York's most famous unsolved crimes.

Human remains left in the Bois de Boulogne, 1981

On the evening of 13 June 1981, a man of Oriental appearance was seen leaving two large suitcases in the Bois de Boulogne before taking to his heels. The witnesses were suspicious and the police were immediately called to the scene. The suitcases were found to contain most of the remains of a young woman, whose body had been cut into pieces and wrapped in plastic rubbish sacks. A bullet was recovered from the base of her skull and traces of semen were found in her sex organs. There was, however, no evidence that she had been raped.

The remains were identified as those of Renée Hartevelt, a twenty-five-year-old Dutch student who had been doing post-graduate work at the Université Censier in Paris. They were found to have been left by Issei Sagawa, a Japanese student at the same college, who lived in the Rue Erlanger, in the sixteenth arrondissement. He had taken the two suitcases to the Bois de Boulogne by taxi on the evening in question, and when police searched his studio apartment they found not only the .22 calibre rifle with which the victim had been shot, but also some other parts of her body, which he had been keeping in his refrigerator.

Sagawa, aged thirty-two, made a confession. He said that Renée Hartevelt, with whom he shared an interest in literature, had visited his apartment on the afternoon of 11 June to help him with some difficult translations, as her French was better than his own. While she was there he asked her to have sexual intercourse with him, but she refused. It was as a result of this rebuff that the murder had taken place.

Sagawa explained, without remorse, that he had killed his fellow-student with a single shot in the back of the

163

neck, and had afterwards pulled off her clothes and had intercourse with the corpse. He had then cut the body into pieces, stopping every now and then to take photographs of it. Those parts which were not put into the suitcases for disposal were kept so that he could eat them, and some had already been consumed. He said that he had wanted to eat a girl's flesh for a long time.

Though all the known facts indicated that this account was true, Sagawa was not tried for the crime. He was, instead, placed under psychiatric observation and later declared to be unfit to stand trial by reason of insanity. He remained in a mental hospital in Paris until May 1984, when he returned to Japan as a result of an agreement between the two countries concerned. This agreement was reached about the same time as the Japanese company Kurita Water Industries, of which Sagawa's father was the president, signed a business deal with a French chemical conglomerate, Elf-Aquitaine.

In Japan, Issei Sagawa entered a mental hospital, where he remained until August 1985. He was then discharged on the hospital superintendent's orders because his 'examination and treatment were finished'. His discharge, however, had been opposed by the hospital's deputy superintendent, Dr Tsuguo Kaneko, who expressed the view that Sagawa was an untreatable psychotic who should have been in prison.

Sagawa, in the meantime, had written a book about the murder of Renée Hartevelt which quickly became a best-seller. Following his discharge from the hospital, he gave a magazine interview, saying that his act of cannibalism had been 'an expression of love', and that he still dreamed of eating a woman's flesh, though without murdering her and only with her consent. He was reported to be staying with his parents in Yokohama.

Housekeeper found dead in Belgravia, 1946

JUNE 14

On 14 June 1946, Detective Inspector James Ball arrived at a house in the Belgravia district of London after being informed that the housekeeper, Miss Elizabeth McLindon, was missing. The house, in Chester Square, was shortly to become the home of the exiled King of Greece, and Miss McLindon, an attractive woman aged forty, had taken up residence there on her own some weeks earlier. It was the king's secretary who had reported her missing.

Miss McLindon's clothes and other belongings were still in the house, but it seemed from the supply of milk outside the back door that she had not been there for six days. However, the door of the library was locked and the key missing; it was therefore necessary for Ball to force it open. When he did so he found the housekeeper's dead body. Miss McLindon had been shot through the back of the neck as she sat at the telephone, evidently about to make a call — and from the condition of the body it appeared that she had been dead for five or six days.

A bullet recovered from the wall and a used cartridge found on the floor had both been fired from a Browning automatic pistol. But the door key was not found there, and there were no signs of a forced entry or a struggle. It seemed that the dead woman had let the culprit into the house herself, and that he had afterwards locked the library door and taken the key away with him.

A search of the housekeeper's bedroom resulted in the discovery of valuable jewellery and a box of letters from various men, all of whom appeared to have been her lovers — and generous ones at that. Two of the letters, both signed 'Arthur', were of particular interest: they had both been posted in Brighton — the first on 11 June, the second

165

the following day — and asked her why she had not been answering the telephone.

As they had both arrived after her death and yet been opened and placed in the bedroom with the others, it was suspected that the murderer had returned to the house in the hope of causing confusion over the date on which the crime had been committed.

Miss McLindon's sister Veronica told the police that 'Arthur' was the dead woman's fiancé, Arthur Boyce, a painter working on Brighton pier. On being questioned, Boyce claimed that he knew nothing of Miss McLindon's death — even though it had been reported in all the newspapers — and that he had been trying to contact her by telephone for several days. But it was learnt from his workmates that he had recently been in possession of a pistol, which he had told them he was going to throw into the sea.

It was also discovered that Arthur Boyce was a convicted bigamist who had served an eighteen-month prison sentence, and that he was wanted for passing dud cheques. One of these cheques — for £135 — had been used to pay for an engagement ring, which the jeweller concerned had recovered from Miss McLindon on 8 June, after the cheque had been returned to him. Boyce was arrested in connection with these offences.

Though Detective Inspector Ball was unable to find the gun with which the murder had been committed, he managed to trace a man named John Rowland, of Caernarvon, who had had a Browning automatic stolen from him while he was sharing lodgings with Boyce in Fulham some months previously.

Rowland was certain that Boyce had taken the gun, and had written to him to ask for it back, but received no reply. An empty cartridge case which had been fired from this gun was produced at Ball's request, and found to have markings indentical to those of the one which had been left in the house in Chester Square.

Arthur Boyce was then charged with murder and brought to trial shortly afterwards. It was believed that he had killed Miss McLindon because she was about to telephone the police after learning that he had paid for her engagement ring with a dud cheque, and that he had afterwards gone to great lengths to conceal his guilt. The jury was much impressed by the ballistics evidence, presented by the famous gunsmith, Robert Churchill, and the prisoner was convicted.

He was hanged on 12 November 1946.

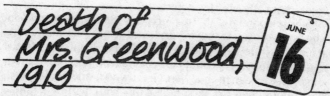

Death of Mrs. Greenwood, 1919

During the early hours of 16 June 1919, Mabel Greenwood, the wife of a solicitor, died at her home in Kidwelly, Carmarthenshire, after an agonizing illness which had started the previous afternoon. Her health had not been good beforehand and her doctor gave the cause of her death as valvular heart disease. But many people suspected that she had been poisoned.

Harold Greenwood, her forty-five-year-old husband, had a practice in nearby Llanelly, but relied upon his wife's private income for the comfort in which they and their four children lived. Unlike his wife, he was not liked in Kidwelly, and a nurse who had attended Mrs Greenwood maintained that there should have been a post-mortem.

Greenwood's marriage, four months later, to Gladys Jones, thirty-one-year-old daughter of one of the proprietors of the *Llanelly Mercury*, gave rise to further rumour and speculation, and the police informed him that they would probably want to have his first wife's body exhumed. He replied that he was agreeable to this, and on 16 April 1920, the exhumation took place.

A post-mortem then revealed that the rumours were justified, for there was no evidence of disease. Instead, arsenic was found in various parts of the body.

A coroner's jury in June found that the deceased had died of arsenic poisoning, and named her husband as the person who had administered the poison. This verdict was applauded by the spectators, and the following day Harold Greenwood was formally charged with murder.

He spent the next four and a half months in prison, and was brought to trial in Carmarthen on 2 November 1920. The case against him then proved to be weaker than the inhabitants of Kidwelly expected.

It was contended by the prosecution that Greenwood, who was known to have purchased a product containing arsenic in June 1917, had poisoned a bottle of wine on the day his wife was taken ill. But while the family's parlour maid gave evidence that Mrs Greenwood, and Mrs Greenwood alone, had drunk some of this wine with her lunch, Irene Greenwood, the defendant's twenty-one-year-old daughter, stated that she, too, had drunk some of it, not only at lunch, but also at supper.

Though another witness claimed that there had been no wine on the table at supper, Irene Greenwood's evidence was enough to raise doubts about the prisoner's guilt. Moreover, these doubts were reinforced by the defence counsel's suggestion that Mrs Greenwood's doctor, an extremely vague person, might have accidentally poisoned her himself.

Harold Greenwood, who had remained calm throughout the trial, was acquitted and left the court a free man. But his legal practice was ruined by the case and he was broken in spirit. He died nine years later, at the age of fifty-five.

Policeman murdered by Barry Prudom, 1982

On 17 June 1982, a policeman was shot dead by a motorist during the course of a routine traffic check near Harrogate in Yorkshire. There were no witnesses to the crime, and there was no apparent motive for it. But as he lay dying, PC David Haigh managed to write the registration number of the culprit's car in his notebook. The killer was then found to be Barry Peter Prudom, a thirty-seven-year-old man already wanted on a wounding charge. His car, a green Citroen, was found abandoned in a field near Leeds.

Prudom, formerly a stable and hard-working man, had had domestic problems for some years, and it seems that they had finally become too much for him. Towards the end of the seventeen-day manhunt which followed he told members of a family which he had taken prisoner: 'I told him (PC Haigh) I'd been sleeping out in the car, and that I didn't think that was an offence. But he said he was going to take me in and got stroppy, so I shot him.' He had, however, given a false name, probably because he feared being arrested for the earlier offence.

After abandoning the car Prudom made his way to Lincolnshire where he broke into a bungalow and robbed an elderly woman of £5, leaving her tied up but unharmed. He then went to Girton, near Newark-on-Trent, where he broke into the home of George Luckett and his wife Sylvia, in search of food and money. George Luckett was shot dead when he tried to defend himself with his own gun; his wife was shot in the head, but survived.

Prudom stole the Luckett's car and drove towards Dalby Forest in north Yorkshire, intending to lie low. But after another shooting, in which a policeman was injured, an intensive search for him was begun. Before long there

169

was a third encounter; this time an unarmed police sergeant was shot three times, the last shot being fired as he lay helpless on the ground.

The search received a great deal of publicity, with much being made of the large number of policemen who were armed and the fact that Prudom had once had SAS training. Another unusual feature of the manhunt was the part played by Eddie McGee, a survival expert called in by the police to track the fugitive.

The taking of the prisoners occurred on the evening of 3 July when Prudom broke into a house in Malton; the victims were Maurice Johnson and his wife, both in their seventies, and their son Brian, aged forty-three. They were held at gunpoint at first, then tied up until Prudom felt that it was safe for him to release them.

He ate and rested in their house, threatening to kill them unless they did as they were told; he also watched television news bulletins and made a voluntary confession of his crimes. When they tried to persuade him to give himself up he refused.

'I'll never let the police take me,' he said. 'I'll kill myself first.'

Early the following morning he left the house and hid in a shelter which he had made by putting wooden boards against a wall. A few hours later Eddie McGee found him and the police started to close in. Prudom immediately began shooting at them. 'Come and get me, you bastards!' he shouted. 'I'll take some of you to hell with me!'

He remained in the shelter as police armed with a variety of weapons took up positions nearby. At 9.30 that Sunday morning an assault was made, with stun-grenades being hurled and rifle-shots fired. Just before 9.40 a.m. Prudom was killed by a bullet which, according to evidence given at the subsequent inquest, was 'almost certainly' fired from his own gun.

He was later found to have sustained twenty-two other injuries during that short series of exchanges which brought Britain's biggest manhunt to an end.

Murder of Mrs. Chung, 1928

JUNE 19

On the afternoon of 19 June 1928, a Chinese couple spending part of their honeymoon in the Lake District village of Grange-in-Borrowdale, left their hotel to go for a walk. Chung Yi Miao, a twenty-eight-year-old doctor of law, and his wealthy twenty-nine-year-old wife had arrived in Grange the previous day after being married in New York a little over a month earlier. They seemed to be happy together.

Some hours later Chung returned for dinner alone, saying that his wife had gone shopping in the nearby town of Keswick. He then remained at the hotel, keeping himself to himself, until finally he began to express anxiety about the lateness of the hour. His wife had still not returned when he decided to go to bed.

Suddenly, at eleven o'clock that night, a police officer called to tell him that his wife was dead.

Mrs Chung's body had been discovered beside a bathing pool a short distance from the hotel; she had been strangled. Her skirt had been pushed up round her waist, and she was lying in such a way as to give the impression that she had been raped or sexually assaulted, though this was later found to have been simulated. Articles of jewellery which had apparently been stolen were discovered — without Chung's knowledge — during a search of the couple's bedroom. They had been deliberately concealed.

Chung Yi Miao was taken into custody on suspicion of murder. At Keswick police station the following morning, having been told nothing about the apparent sex offence and robbery, he convinced the police of his guilt by remarking, 'It is terrible — my wife assaulted, robbed and murdered!' Despite uncertainty about his motive for the crime, he was

171

formally charged and brought to trial at the Carlisle Assizes in November the same year.

Chung denied the offence, and the trial lasted three days. The evidence offered by the prosecution was entirely circumstantial — the defendant's knowledge of the state in which the body had been found, the jewellery hidden in the hotel bedroom, the fact that the cord used to murder Mrs Chung was of the same type as used in the hotel, and so on. The motive now suggested was thwarted sexual desire.

In his defence it was stated that two unknown men of Oriental appearance had been following the couple, the suggestion being that *they* could have murdered Mrs Chung after the defendant had left her. An attempt was also made to show that Chung's accent had caused misunderstandings. For example, he denied that in referring to his wife's body, on the night that he was informed of her death, he had asked, 'Had she knickers on?' What he had really asked, he said, was, 'Had she necklace on?'

The jury was not impressed by all this and found the case proved; Chung was sentenced to death. Following an unsuccessful appeal, which he conducted himself, he was hanged at Strangeways Prison, Manchester, on 6 December 1928.

It was afterwards suggested that the real reason for the murder was Chung's discovery, just after their marriage, that his wife would not be able to have children.

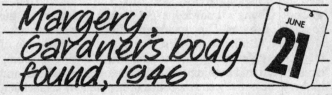

Margery Gardner's body found, 1946

JUNE 21

During the early afternoon of 21 June 1946, the body of Margery Gardner, aged thirty-two, was found in a hotel

172

bedroom in the Notting Hill district of London. She had died from suffocation, though only after being subjected to a number of sadistic acts: while alive, she had been whipped, her nipples almost bitten off and a rough instrument rotated in her vagina, causing much bleeding. After washing blood from her face, her murderer had covered her body up to the neck with bedclothes. He had left the curtains drawn.

Margery Gardner was a married woman, separated from her husband; she spent much of her time drinking and dancing and occasionally worked as a film extra. On the night of 20 June she had been to the Panama Club in South Kensington in the company of Neville Heath, a twenty-nine-year-old former RAF officer with a criminal record for housebreaking, theft and fraud. He had afterwards taken her to the hotel by taxi.

The police were certain that Heath was the person responsible for the murder, and released his name and description to the press, saying that they wanted him 'to assist them with their inquiries'. On 24 June they received a letter from him, posted in Worthing, in which he claimed to be innocent of the crime.

'I booked in at the hotel last Sunday, but not with Mrs Gardner, whom I met for the first time during the week,' he wrote. 'I had drinks with her on Friday evening, and whilst I was with her she met an acquaintance with whom she was obliged to sleep. The reasons, as I understand them, were mainly financial.

'It was then that Mrs Gardner asked if she could use my hotel room until two o'clock and intimated that, if I returned after that, I might spend the remainder of the night with her. I gave her my keys and told her to leave the hotel door open.

'It must have been almost 3 a.m. when I returned to the hotel and found her in the condition of which you are aware. I realised I was in an invidious position, and rather than notify the police I packed my belongings and left.'

He said that he was using a false name, but could be

contacted through the personal column of the *Daily Telegraph*. He also said that he had the instrument with which Mrs Gardner had been beaten and would be forwarding it to them. It never arrived.

The police continued their search for him, circulating copies of a photograph to every force in the country. On 6 July he went to Bournemouth police station, calling himself Group Captain Rupert Brooke, in connection with the disappearance of twenty-one-year-old Doreen Marshall, who was believed to have had dinner with him on the evening of 3 July. He was recognized and held for questioning by officers of the Metropolitan Police. On 8 July he was taken by car to London, where he was later charged with the murder of Margery Gardner.

About the time the charge was made the body of Doreen Marshall was found in Branksome Chine, a wooded valley about a mile from the hotel in which Heath had been staying in Bournemouth. Like Margery Gardner, she was naked and had various injuries. In this case, however, the victim had died as a result of deep knife-wounds in her throat, and had been mutilated afterwards.

Though Heath was charged with this second murder, his trial, which began at the Old Bailey on 24 September, concerned only the first. A defence of insanity was made on his behalf, his counsel seeking to establish that his long history of petty crime was proof of instability. Heath, however, appeared indifferent to it all. On being found guilty, he had nothing to say; on being sentenced to death, he made no appeal. He showed no sign of remorse and made no confession.

'My only regret at leaving the world is that I have been damned unworthy of you both,' he wrote to his parents.

Neville Heath was hanged at Pentonville Prison on 26 October 1946.

Murder of Mrs. Parker, 1954

On the afternoon of 22 June 1954, Mrs Honora Parker, a middle-aged woman, was beaten to death in a park in Canterbury, New Zealand, by two teenage girls, one of whom was her own daughter. The girls attacked her with a brick wrapped in a stocking, striking forty-five blows — twenty-four of them to their victim's head and face — before running to a nearby teashop to raise the alarm. But nobody was taken in by their story that Mrs Parker had been killed when she slipped and fell on the pavement, and soon they admitted the truth. Pauline Parker, aged sixteen, and her friend Juliet Hulme, fifteen, were therefore charged with murder.

The two girls were found to have had a lesbian relationship which had been a matter of concern to the parents of both. Mrs Parker had been determined to put a stop to it, but had failed to do so. Then, early in 1954, Mr Hulme decided to take Juliet to South Africa. Pauline declared that she would go, too, regardless of the opposition of her own parents. The idea of murdering her mother seems to have occurred to her about the same time. 'Why could not mother die?' she wrote in her diary on 13 February. 'Dozens of people, thousands of people, are dying every day. So why not mother, and father too?'

A later entry, written two days before the crime took place, showed that both girls had given the idea a lot of thought. 'We discussed our plans for moidering mother and made them a little clearer,' Pauline recorded. 'I want it to appear either a natural or an accidental death.'

Pauline Parker and Juliet Hulme were brought to trial in Christchurch, both apparently unrepentant. The court was given details of their sex life and various fantasies in which they had jointly indulged, the defence contending that their crime had been the result of 'paranoia of the exalted type', and that they were both certifiably mad. To the prosecution, however, they were 'highly intelligent and perfectly sane, but precocious and dirty-minded girls', who had committed a 'callously planned and premeditated murder'.

The jury agreed with the prosecution, and the prisoners were found guilty and sentenced to be detained during Her Majesty's pleasure. But this proved not to be a very harsh sentence, for they were both released in 1958.

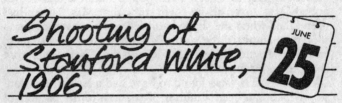

Shooting of Stanford White, 1906

JUNE 25

On 25 June 1906, Stanford White, a distinguished architect aged fifty-two, became the victim of a sensational shooting during the first performance of a new farce at the Madison Square Roof Garden Theatre in New York. In the middle of the play he was suddenly shot dead by Harry Thaw, a thirty-four-year-old millionaire playboy. He fell to the floor and died instantly, one of Thaw's three bullets having entered his brain.

Thaw, on being arrested, admitted responsibility for White's death, but claimed that it had been a justified act. He said that his wife, a former model and chorus girl, had been seduced by the victim some years earlier, and that in such a case an 'unwritten law' allowed the husband to avenge the wrong which his wife had suffered. He was charged with murder.

Thaw was the son of a railroad magnate. Born in Pennsylvania, he had inherited his father's wealth while